D1353519

The

BRITISH WORLD AIRLINES

Story

MIDLAND PUBLISHING LIMITED

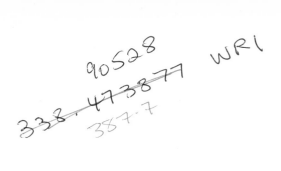

Published by
Midland Publishing Limited
24 The Hollow, Earl Shilton
Leicester, LE9 7NA, England
Tel: 01455 847 815
Fax: 01455 841 805

ISBN 1 85780 043 5

Edited by Ken Ellis

Design concept and layout
© Midland Publishing Limited and
Stephen Thompson Associates, 1996.

Printed in England by
Clearpoint Colourprint Limited
Salop Street, Daybrook
Nottingham, NG5 6HD

With special thanks to:
Aero International (Regional);
Roy Bonser, George Burton and
Malcolm Ginsberg.

Photographs from the archives of
British World Airlines and the author.
With special thanks to George Pennick
and Glen Sweeney.

Other photographic contributors are
credited with their work.

**Front cover: Fleet development 1946-96.
The BAe 146, has been part of the fleet
since 1991, although BAF undertook route
proving for the type in 1982.**
Glen Sweeney / British World

**Inset: Silver City started operations in
1946 with Avro Lancastrians, an airline
version of the Lancaster bomber.**
via Mike Hooks

**Title page: In 1996 British World were
operating a fleet of five BAC One-Eleven
500 series.** Glen Sweeney / British World

**We hope that you enjoy reading
this book . . .**

Midland Publishing titles are carefully
edited and designed by a knowledgeable and enthusiastic team of specialists, with many years experience.

Further titles are in the course of
preparation but we would welcome
ideas on what you would like to see.

In addition, our associate company,
Midland Counties Publications, offers
an exceptionally wide range of aviation, spaceflight, astronomy, military,
naval and transport books and videos
for sale by mail-order around the
world.

For a copy of the appropriate catalogue, or to order further copies of this
book, and any of the titles mentioned
on this or the next page, please write,
telephone or fax to:

Midland Counties Publications
Unit 3 Maizefield,
Hinckley Fields
Hinckley, Leics. England
LE10 1YF

Tel: 01455 233 747
Fax: 01455 233 737

THE
BRITISH WORLD AIRLINES
STORY

BRITISH WORLD AIRLINES
1946 - 1996

Foreword

ifty years in any business is a long time. In aviation terms the list of airlines surviving half a century is short, a matchless catalogue of world famous names. British World has now joined that unique band.

Over the years British World has changed its course (and its title from time to time) as dictated by market forces. Today it is the last truly independent specialist airline of any size in the United Kingdom, self-sufficient in all areas and a major charter airline in the European scene.

Having been with the airline since 1977, I have seen many changes and in particular with aircraft type, starting with the Carvair, progressing through the Dart Herald, Viscount, HS.125, BAC One-Eleven, BAe 146 plus a new order in 1996 for two ATR.72s. In earlier years, the airline had to work with aircraft that either nobody wanted or had come to the end of their perceived working life, but the company always managed to get the best out of them, regularly returning an operating profit.

Much of this success can be attributed to the British World workforce who have always been known for their dedicated hard work, flexibility and being able to respond to a business opportunity with enthusiasm and pride in their work. Above all their loyalty and ability more than anything else shapes and styles the character of our company and our collective aim is to provide the highest standard of service available anywhere and deliver a product second to none in aviation terms.

I feel privileged to have learned so much in my aviation career from a company such as British World and from the people associated with the airline over the last 20 years, many of these people employed for longer than myself. The company has an enviable record of low turnover of personnel which has resulted in high retained expertise.

I am sure others in the industry will agree with me that there is nothing quite like aviation and the opportunities of learning something new everyday still exist which makes every working day a challenge.

The British World Airlines Board of Directors, left to right:
Colin Smale-Saunders, Engineering Director; John Deether, Financial Director;
Robert Sturman, Chairman; Mike Sessions, Sales Director;
Captain Ian Vanderbeek, Operations Director.

Thanks go to British World Airlines and its predecessors for the opportunity.

I commend this illustrated life story of the first 50 years of British World Airlines as a piece of aviation history.

Here's to the next fifty years!

Mike Sessions
Sales Director
British World Airlines

Introduction

$\mathcal{A}$s life returned to normality after the end of the Second World War, the ban on civil flying was lifted on 31st December 1945, a day eagerly awaited by the industry. Unfortunately, although it allowed operators to undertake charter work, it came as a shock to the fledgling airlines to learn that no new scheduled services would be authorised. In the past few months since the general election of 5th July 1945 that brought in Clement Attlee's Labour government, the word 'nationalisation' had become fashionable, with the result that such activities were to be handled by the newly-created state airline, British European Airways Corporation (BEAC), which had joined the previously-established international long haul flag carrier, British Overseas Airways Corporation (BOAC).

Most of the newcomers had been founded by ex-RAF personnel with the memory of free flying still fresh and 'demob' money burning a hole in the pockets of their standard issue suits. Almost all employed former military machines for the *ad hoc* charter work, since they were available in large numbers as the RAF disposed of its surplus stocks for a nominal sum.

By the spring of 1948 scheduled services remained relatively few in number, with the flag carrier still unable to cope with any major expansion. As a result, some of the independent companies were invited to operate the dormant pre-war routes, as well as to introduce new sectors. It was an opportunity that was welcomed enthusiastically even with the knowledge that the crumbs of comfort from this slight relaxation of official policy would be thinly scattered.

New shape for 1996, the first of two ATR.72-210s ready for delivery. AI(R)

The overall picture of the UK airline activities in the late 1940s was therefore not very encouraging. While the majority of the newcomers were financially dependent on charters and the seasonal scheduled market, a few were much more ambitious. One such company was Silver City, probably one of the best known British airlines of that era. From small beginnings it progressed through the years via take-overs and mergers to become a part of British United Airways, leading eventually to British Air Ferries and British World Airlines. While the latter was only formally created on 6th April 1993, it can nevertheless trace its history back 50 years via a number of long defunct carriers to the early uncertain post-war days.

Half a century is a long time to survive in the airline business and is an achievement equalled by few. British World Airlines can rightly claim this distinction.

Alan J Wright
Epping, Essex   April 1996

Silver City

After the nose and tail cones were added to the Avro Lancaster, the resulting Lancastrian airliner had attractive lines for its peacetime role. Silver City's trio were painted in a simple livery and carried the company's crest on the nose.
via Mike Hooks

Throughout 1946 charter companies continued to spring up all over the country. With so many ex-RAF aircraft available at low prices, many were encouraged to join what promised to be the post-war boom in air travel. By necessity, the majority of the newcomers had to be content with operating a couple of demobbed de Havilland Dominies or Airspeed Oxfords that had been transformed into Rapides and Consuls respectively, there being few suitable new types available. The Avro Lancastrian, a civil version of the wartime Lancaster bomber, was almost out of reach for all but the state-owned carriers, but there were two exceptions, one being Skyways, the other Silver City Airways.

Silver City was formally registered on 25th November 1946, but from the outset it differed from the multitude by possessing a board of directors with vast experience of company affairs. A link was also forged with British Aviation Services (BAS), an organisation formed a year earlier to provide a consultancy facility together with maintenance and limited aircraft operations. It became responsible for the general administration of Silver City, a task no doubt aided by the fact that the companies had the same managing director, namely Air Commodore G J Powell, a pre-war Imperial Airways pilot and a senior member of Transport Command during the war.

One of the main reasons for forming the airline was to provide a regular link with Australia, a route flown by BOAC and Qantas, but with limited capacity available. As a result, financial backing was forthcoming from mining interests in the UK and Australia to allow the industry's personnel to be readily transferred without the delays caused by fully booked commercial flights. The choice of the airline's name was influenced by the Zinc Corporation's mining activities in the area of Broken Hill, New South Wales. This town was already known as 'The Silver City', so the airline's backers decided to adopt the title for the new venture.

While these formalities were underway, consideration had been given to the equipment necessary to fulfil the airline's purpose. Certainly something fast and reliable was essential, which limited the choice to a large degree. The only type meeting these requirements and readily available was the Lancastrian, so an order was placed with Avro for three new Mk.3s, all of which were delivered by October. Allocated the registrations G-AHBT, 'BV and 'BW, it was the latter which was entrusted with the company's inaugural operation towards the end of November with a trip to and from Johannesburg, but it was not long before similar charters were arranged to keep the trio busily employed around the world.

While Silver City managed to attract several senior staff members from the State airlines, most of the flight crew were ex-RAF with considerable experience of the more belligerent Lancaster. In those days the type appeared enormous and seemed to justify the need for two pilots, navigator, radio operator and a steward. Passengers quickly came to appreciate the standard offered by the Lancastrians and the crews. Even 50 years ago the myth existed that the national carrier could not be surpassed in terms of comfort and service. This was soon disproved by Silver City which provided 13 adjustable seats with a centre aisle, together with a high standard of catering and support services.

Those expecting anything different forgot that in those early stages of development after the war, none of the British charter airlines could justify the expense of its own steps, ground units and the many other items used by handlers; there was a common supply of such equipment for all operators. Likewise the meals on offer while airborne originated at the same catering source. It was therefore only the smile of the cabin crew member that could perhaps identify the airline!

Despite every attempt to make the journey as comfortable as possible, the trip from the UK to Australia was still a daunting experience with the four Rolls-Royce Merlins droning away hour after hour. Even the first leg to Malta took six hours, followed by a one hour rest for refuelling before the next sector to Basra, which consumed another nine hours.

Although the Lancastrian did not remain with Silver City beyond the beginning of 1949, it proved to be an excellent aircraft for the duties entrusted to it, at the same time helping to establish the company. The type continued in service with other carriers, but by 1952 after a relatively short career, all examples had been withdrawn or had crashed, the latter fate being suffered by at least 16 of those produced.

Initially the airline selected Langley, near Slough, as its headquarters, but its proximity to Heathrow quickly ended the career of this airfield, which like so many since, is now but a memory. In any case, in early 1947 Silver City found it more useful to transplant itself to Blackbushe, near Camberley, where British Aviation Services had already settled down sometime earlier. By the middle of the year Silver City had

added a number of Douglas DC-3s (in the shape of former RAF Dakota IIIs) to its fleet, which began to fly *ad hoc* passenger and freight charters.

Although the aircraft were intended to perform on short haul sectors, the urgent need for mercy flights in India meant that one of the machines was despatched to assist in the movement of Hindus from Pakistan. It was at this time that the company first became associated with the Bristol Freighter, the aircraft for which Silver City is probably best remembered.

It was in 1944 that the Bristol Type 170 evolved as a short haul, general duty freighter for military use. The rugged structural design was thought ideal for support work in the Burma campaign, but before the construction of the machine was completed, the war was over and jungle operations were thankfully no longer necessary. The manufacturer therefore turned to the civil market which soon indicated that there was a future for such a utility freight and passenger transport.

Silver City was one interested company, so it decided to evaluate the aircraft by leasing an example from the manufacturer for European duties, but in the event it was sent to India to assist the DC-3 in its enormous task. Although built as a Wayfarer, with 32 passenger seats, all the seats were removed for the purposes of this operation, which meant that the hapless evacuees had to sit on the floor surrounded by their strictly weight limited luggage.

During its stay on the airlift, the Wayfarer was responsible for moving the greatest number of refugees, carrying over 1,100 passengers in nine days. Loads were kept within the operating limits of the type, but even while observing the rules it was still able to carry a total of 151 travellers during the course of a single day. Needless to say, the relief organisation and the airline were very impressed by the aircraft's performance.

A trio of Silver City's Freighter Mk 21s (including G-AIME) parked at Lydd in 1963, having been withdrawn from use to await scrapping.
Mike Hooks

Bristol Freighter Mk 21 G-AIFM 'City of Carlisle' joined Silver City in 1951 and was operated until shortly after the creation of BUAF in January 1963. It was scrapped at Southend at the end of the year.
via George Pennick

Freighter Mk 32 G-ANWM began its car
ferry career with Silver City in July 1956,
later being transferred to British United in
January 1963. Named 'City of Aberdeen',
it carries the last letter of its registration
in a circle on the nose.
Author

CAR FERRIES

In common with many other UK charter companies, Silver City applied for approval to operate a summer scheduled service to Jersey in 1948 with a DC-3. In those days the Channel Islands' routes were considered 'bread and butter' operations and much sought after. A far more significant event took place on 13th July, at Lympne Airport in Kent when it acted as the departure point for the first cross-Channel car ferry by air. Silver City used the prototype Freighter G-AGVC to fly the 42 miles to Le Touquet, the French airfield chosen for its convenient position and accessibility. On the occasion of the inaugural trip only one car was carried, this being an Armstrong Siddeley Lancaster, a rather appropriate choice bearing in mind the airline's association with the Avro version. The flying time was a mere 25 minutes for the sector, but it confirmed that the scheme was practical and likely to become popular judging by the level of interest generated. For the rest of the summer the flights were operated on a charter basis. In the three months of operation, the airline carried 180 vehicles across the water.

It was, of course, an era when car ownership was comparatively rare, but the favoured few were becoming increasingly keen of motoring to the fashionable French resorts. Prior to the air services, ships provided the only means of transport, few of which were suitable for the task. As late as 1953 it was still necessary to load vehicles by crane at Dover until the new ferry terminal was available. This enabled ships with stern doors to be introduced, but this still involved the vessel reversing into dock at both ports followed by difficult shunting operations by the vehicle drivers.

There was plenty of scope for an alternative, and encouraged by the results of its short programme, Silver City decided to increase the size of the venture in 1949 by making it a scheduled service. This entailed making an application to BEA for an associate agreement licence, but since the flag carrier had little interest in car ferries, approval was quickly forthcoming.

The first departure of the new season was flown on 13th April, but at the time there was little to indicate whether the services would be patronised by the travelling public. The company did not have long to wait. After only two weeks bookings began to accelerate to such an extent that the number of flights had to be increased from four per day in May, to 16 per day in the July and August peak periods. The busiest day of the year was 28th July

when 23 round trips were made by the four Freighters in use, one operated by the British carrier's French partner, *Société Commerciale Aérienne du Littoral*. After the summer season had ended, the frequency was steadily reduced until the schedules were flown when customers appeared at the terminal. Not only had well over 2,500 cars and their passengers been flown, but so had 50 motorcycles and five pedal cycles complete with riders. The latter were charged £2 and a further £1 for their trusty steeds.

While cars were winging their way across the English Channel, elsewhere a more serious airlift was in progress. Berlin was under siege by the Russians with the result that a major operation was mounted to ferry food, fuel and other essentials by air. All suitable aircraft were employed, resulting in Silver City detaching three Freighters to Germany, the only twin-engined British civil aircraft taking part in the operation. They proved invaluable for the transportation of bulky cargo, flying over 600 hours during the course of 213 sorties.

During the years from 1950 to 1953 the car ferry business continued to flourish with records constantly broken. Nevertheless, aircraft utilisation, even in the busiest times, rarely exceeded three hours per day, the equivalent of nine single trips. In an attempt to reduce turn-around times, the airline designed a motor-powered loading ramp with a 2hp JAP engine providing the motive power. Four of these units were produced, two for use at each terminal.

Since the Freighters could only accommodate two cars on each trip, an aircraft with greater capacity would obviously be useful to increase productivity. As a possible solution, Silver City requested the manufacturer to develop a larger variant. This soon led to the Mk 32 which possessed a nose extended by 5ft to carry a third car, together with a 23-seat passenger cabin in the rear. Known as the Superfreighter by the airline, the first of six was delivered in March 1953, but these were quickly followed by repeat orders until a total of 17 various versions of the Freighter were on strength. Several new routes had already been launched, including Southampton-Cherbourg and the airline's first Belgian venture using Southend as the UK gateway for a link with Ostend.

At the end of the 1953 summer season Silver City was able to announce that it had flown the staggering number of 38,000 vehicles in the first ten months, easily exceeding the previous year's total of nearly 10,500. The Freighter 32's extra capacity certainly helped to produce these figures, but the airline continued to consider larger types for the ferry services. One such machine was the French Breguet Br 761S *Deux Ponts*, a truly double-deck machine with equal volume of space in both upper and lower areas. An early specimen was leased from the French manufacturer for three months and duly despatched to Hamburg for employment on the company's cargo runs to Berlin. Such was its lifting ability that it replaced three Freighters, all of which returned to Britain for car ferry duties. Although the *Deux Ponts* proved very satisfactory, the airline returned it at the end of its lease period with no further action taken. The Blackburn Beverley was also viewed favourably, but the manufacturer could not offer early deliveries due to the RAF order, so any thoughts about acquiring the type were quietly dropped.

Silver City decided to continue with its worthy Freighter fleet, but there was a growing concern about the state of its main operating base at Lympne. The somewhat modest grass-covered airfield had begun life in 1917, ironically as a ferry base for military aircraft leaving the country for France. Between the wars light aircraft provided the bulk of the activity until the RAF took possession again in 1939. It then became a popular target for the *Luftwaffe* which dropped some 1,400 bombs on the airfield, 90 of them landing on buildings.

The post-war tranquillity was shattered in 1948 with the launch of the ferry flights, which thereafter continuously pounded the grass surface with little respite even in the winter months. In early 1953 operations had to be suspended following a number of aircraft becoming stuck in the mud created by earlier movements. This necessitated a temporary move to Southend, Essex, with the airline continuing to bring the matter to the Ministry of Civil Aviation's attention as owner of the airfield. Similar problems manifested themselves every time there was heavy rain, which in 1953 was quite frequent in that so-called summer. Finally, there was sufficient precipitation to close the facility once again, this time forcing Silver City to transfer its operations to West Malling, which was at least on the same side of the Thames!

It was a situation which could not be tolerated since it affected the carrier's reputation for reliability that had been built up since 1948. It was pointed out that Silver City had paid thousands of pounds in landing fees and was by far the Ministry's best cus-tomer. Needless to say, it had very little effect upon the administrators in Whitehall, so without further ado, the airline announced that it proposed to build its own airport which would be designed to handle car ferry operations. The site chosen was northeast of Lydd, Kent, a flat area consisting mainly of shingle, sand and clay. Design studies began in October with work starting a couple months later after formal approval of the plans.

Much local material was used in the construction of the two runways, which were initially 3,600ft and 3,300ft in length. A suitable terminal building was provided, while Customs and immigration were housed in a building separated from the main structure by a passageway for the use of incoming traffic, with a similar arrangement for outbound vehicles. Remarkably, the entire project was completed in seven months to become Britain's first civil airport to be built since the Second World War. Ferryfield, as the new base was appropriately named, began its operational life on 13th July 1954. At first only the Le Touquet route was flown, but such destinations as Calais and Ostend were soon added. A start then began on winding down the services still operating from Lympne, the final departure being flown on 3rd October using the same Freighter that had started the enterprise six years or so earlier. Subsequently, the Ferryfield was extended in 1957 to permit the handling of a greater number of passengers then being generated by the non-ferry movements.

Expansion of services continued with the introduction of new sectors including a couple across the Irish Sea. First of these to be started linked Stranraer (Castle Kennedy) with Belfast (Newtownards), a distance of 35 miles. The flight was about 18 minutes, so including the loading and unloading processes, the overall elapsed time for the trip was some 35 minutes, a marked improvement on the frequently unpleasant Irish Sea journeys. Fares were set at a rate comparable with the established south coast operation, resulting in a car 12ft 6in long being charged £7 for the single trip and passengers a mere £2/10/0 (£2.50).

Silver City's traffic figures improved each year with a record number of more than 56,000 vehicles becoming airborne in 1955 compared with 42,500 one year earlier. By the time that the tenth anniversary of the ferry was reached, this annual figure had climbed to over 70,000 with services as popular as ever. During the period since the 1948 launch, the airline had carried 215,000 cars,

The first Freighter Mk 32 was registered G-AMWA and was developed at the request of Silver City, entering service in March 1953. The extended nose allowed a greater car/passenger combination.
via Author

70,000 motor and pedal cycles together with 759,000 passengers on 125,000 flights. One of the attractions was without doubt the willingness of the company to pass on any savings in the form of reduced fares. Following a substantial drop in the 1958 tariffs, advance bookings reached 30,000 by April compared with 14,000 for the same period in the previous year.

Later in the 1950s Silver City experienced another bout of airfield problems, this time Southampton/Eastleigh being the culprit. As at Lympne, the rain-soaked grass surface could not cope with the frequent visits by the laden Freighters, so the Cherbourg and Channel Islands' services were transferred to Bournemouth on a temporary basis. The Guernsey sector had been introduced partly to fly flowers and garden produce back to the mainland, with vehicles normally carried outbound. The rather restrictive licence specified that only six passengers could be carried per day on the service, which was operated in competition with Jersey Airlines. With the exception of these difficulties, the cross-Channel ferry services continued as before, with the Freighters relentlessly trundling backwards and forwards across the narrow stretch of water at an average altitude of about 2,000ft.

A slight change of policy was becoming apparent by the end of the decade, when preparations began to counter the anticipated competition from surface transport. The company decided to increase the number of longer routes rather than concentrate all the resources on the traditional short sectors between England and France. Applications were submitted for licences to serve several points on the continent, at the same time adding various UK regional airports to the list of possible departure points for the ferry flights.

Silver City was also actively engaged in evaluating types with which to replace the existing fleet, a typical example being the Handley Page HPR.8. This project had an obvious relationship with the Herald, but at the same time had the general configuration of the Freighter. Powered by two Rolls-Royce Dart turboprops, the aircraft was designed to carry six cars, two-abreast on the same floor level, with the flight deck positioned above. When employed for vehicle ferry work its aft cabin was designed to accommodate up to 30 travellers, but if laid out for short haul, high-density passenger operations, about 100 seats could be installed. A dedicated airliner version was to have been fitted with an observation lounge in the nose.

Whichever type was finally selected, the airline calculated that it would need ten, but inevitably it required considerable financial investment at a time when the future prospects looked less assured. The company was saved from the dilemma by a series of mergers and re-organisations in the early 1960s which also provided the answer to the re-equipment problem.

Interestingly, at this stage the concern about the stronger competition from the water-borne ferries seemed to be taking second place to the probable effects of the proposed Channel tunnel. The latter scheme had been revived once again and assuming the necessary approval was received, it was due to become operational in 1970. History has shown that it was to be more than another 20 years before this became a reality, by which time air ferries were but a memory anyway.

In the event it was in 1964 that the first major advances were made by the sea ferries when the Norwegian Thoresen line introduced ships with opening bow and stern doors on to the Channel run to give a true roll-on/roll-off (Ro-Ro) facility. Although new on these routes, this device had been incorporated in the numerous ferries operating on the domestic Danish and Swedish services for some time. The benefits were considerable and no doubt accelerated the decline of the air ferries, although another ten years or so passed before they finally became extinct.

SCHEDULES AND CHARTERS

Whilst the car ferry business played a large part in Silver City's activities, the company did not rely entirely on this market for its existence. Indeed, the airline's early operations revolved around its Lancastrians, but it was not long before the Zinc Corporation and its mining associates found that an 'in-house' airline was no longer

needed. Ownership passed to British Aviation Services (itself owned by the P&O Shipping Group) which acquired the entire share holding, a transaction which brought little obvious change to the airline's operations, but was to pave the way for some future expansion.

Air Kruise was the first company to join the Group, a logical step because it already possessed a base at Lympne and operated scheduled services with DH Rapides. These were soon replaced by DC-3s and the network was increased considerably by the addition of new routes. During the summer season, Air Kruise's aircraft could be found at numerous continental airports while employed on inclusive tour (IT) charters. In fact, the company was one of the earliest operators of this now familiar form of business. With the completion of Ferryfield, the carrier transferred its services from Lympne, at the same time adding a number of prominent tour operators to its list of clients. After remaining autonomous for a number of years within the British Aviation Services Group, Air Kruise's operations were taken over by Silver City in 1958 and the aircraft absorbed into the latter's fleet.

A couple of years earlier the Group had acquired Lancashire Aircraft Corporation, Manx Airlines and Dragon Airways, all companies located in the north of England. Of these, Lancashire was one of the earliest and largest of the post-war carriers, initially operating a fleet of converted Handley Page Halifaxes, replaced in due course by a equally large number of Avro Yorks. These maintained a steady flow of contract charters for the Air Ministry, carrying thousands of military personnel to and from the Middle East. In those days London's future third airport at Stansted was used as the UK terminal, in addition to housing the engineering facilities for the four-engined fleet.

Manx and Dragon both operated Rapides for scheduled services, although larger and more modern equipment was beginning to be employed at the time of the re-organisation. During 1957 the trio were combined to create the northern division of Silver City with its base established at Blackpool. Scheduled services were flown with a growing number of DC-3s, together with DH Herons and Wayfarers.

Silver City already employed a Wayfarer to maintain a Ferryfield-Le Touquet coach/air/rail service known as the 'Silver Arrow', this link accounting for only 20 minutes of the overall 6 hours 50

Magnificent Handley Page Hermes G-ALDU taxying at Gatwick, April 1962. It was transferred from Britavia to Silver City in July 1959 and used for inclusive tour charters, trooping and the 'Silver Arrow' service to Le Touquet before being withdrawn and scrapped at Southend in October 1962.
George Pennick

minutes journey from London to Paris. A similar procedure was adopted for a Brussels 'Silver Arrow' operation, although in this case the Belgian leg was completed by coach, giving a city centre to city centre overall time of 7 hours 40 minutes. To cope with the demand during 1958, the carrier converted one of its long-nosed Freighters with a 60-seat, all-passenger layout to become a Super Wayfarer. Already well supported by those not in a hurry to reach the French capital, 1959 brought a significant change to the operation.

Before 1954, Silver City's parent company had not actually operated aircraft in its own name, but having been successful in its tender for a series of trooping flights, Britavia (the trading name of British Aviation Services) purchased six Handley Page Hermes from BOAC. After much industrial strife, the first of the machines was delivered to the airline's Blackbushe base to allow

the first sortie to be flown in the company's livery during July 1954. In addition to fulfilling the military contracts, the Hermes were used extensively for IT charters for a number of years, but by June 1959 the general decline in troop movements caused the airline to transfer the remaining fleet members to Silver City. At the same time the opportunity was taken to move the operating base from Blackbushe, an airport long under threat of closure. Ferryfield was unable to cope with any more traffic, especially that likely to be generated by the 68-seat airliners, so the 'Silver Arrow' service transferred to Manston ready for the inaugural trip on 15th June.

This time travellers had a train journey on the recently-electrified line between Victoria and Margate, with coaches providing the connecting link with the airport. Onward travel in France was similar but used chartered diesel railcars for the sector to Paris. The change added a few miles to the flight, but it was still a very short trip for an aircraft previously employed on long haul work to the Middle and Far East. Until a year before, Manston had been occupied by a USAF fighter unit and was still under Air Ministry control, so the facilities for the civilian customers were somewhat basic. Throughout the next year the 'Silver Arrow' service continued to attract healthy loads for the Hermes, which were also fully utilised on IT flights to the holiday spots just beginning to come within the reach of a growing number of British holidaymakers.

To further improve the 'Silver Arrow' operation, every effort was made to persuade the French to build a two mile rail spur into Le Tou-quet to link with main system. Eventually the negotiations were successful, but the agreement reached meant that the UK company transferred three Superfreighters to the *Compagnie Air Transport*, giving the latter (of which French Railways was the majority shareholder) the right to operate vehicle ferry flights into both Ferryfield and Bournemouth. These developments were sufficient to galvanise the French authorities into action and they commenced work to restore the airport to it pre-war state, although it was doubtless recalled that the Allies were responsible for its destruction in June 1944 anyway!

Work proceeded apace on a new terminal building and car handling facilities, while, for

Hermes G-ALDG became a cabin trainer at Gatwick in turn with BUA and British Caledonian. It is now preserved by the Duxford Aviation Society.
Ken Ellis collection

good measure, the runway was also extended so that the Hermes could be safely operated. Later, Silver City decided to expand its network of schedules from northern England, some of them intended to be extensions of the 'Silver Arrow' services. These flights were planned to be operated by leased Vickers Viscounts, but before the operation could be launched in early 1962, the company came under new ownership which had different ideas.

As a consequence, the Hermes fleet was moved from Manston to Gatwick before the start of the summer season to operate ITs and trooping flights from the new location. This change also affected the 'Silver Arrow' because the well established service was uprooted yet again, this time with its UK departure point at Gatwick and employing Viscounts in British United Airways (BUA) livery. The Silver City title was carried by the Hermes until the end of the summer whereupon the survivors were retired and in due course scrapped.

One example was retained at Gatwick as a cabin trainer for BUA, later passing to British

Caledonian for the same purpose and each time adopting the livery of its new 'operator'. The fuselage of this machine (G-ALDG) went on to be preserved by the Duxford Aviation Society, as part of their collection of British-built airliners, at the Imperial War Museum's airfield at Duxford, near Cambridge. Although G-ALDG today wears BOAC livery and is but a fuselage, it is a unique survivor of a class of airliner that would otherwise be extinct.

Surprisingly, the Silver City title was revived briefly in 1973 when Air Holdings decided to create a carrier using the well-known name. Earlier it had acquired Air Canada's Vickers Vanguard fleet which had been traded in to Lockheed in part payment for their new TriStar widebodies. Three of the large turboprop types were unsold, so it was decided to operate them for passenger and cargo charters instead of letting them lie idle. The venture did not last beyond the end of the year when the fleet was sold and the Silver City name finally disappeared into history.

Air Bridges

British World's other principal forebear was Air Charter, a carrier formed at Croydon in 1947 by F A Laker, many years later better known as Sir Freddie Laker and for his battles with authorities. The airline operated a motley collection of elderly machines to carry out passenger and freight charters, but since business was not too brisk, he also formed a maintenance organisation at Southend known as Aviation Traders. With so many surplus military aircraft readily available, the company proceeded to convert them for civil use or break them for spares. This activity was particularly useful during the course of the Berlin Airlift which became the benefactor of many struggling British airlines. Aviation Traders took no active part in the operation, but instead it supplied other carriers with suitable equipment. When the airlift was over, most of the participating machines were scrapped, but during their short, but valuable, careers they had provided the airlines with the means for survival.

In the meantime, Air Charter had found the air transport market to be very bleak, so it wisely decided to dispose of its fleet and await more promising conditions. In early 1951 the company took over Surrey Flying Services, which was operating freight charters with an Avro York. Later in the same year, the Blackbushe-based Fairflight was also acquired, thereby adding an Avro Tudor to the collection.

Equally useful was the valuable freight contract held by the carrier which called for regular flights between Hamburg and Berlin. This second, but oft-forgotten airlift, gradually expanded with an increase in the number of aircraft and sorties flown each week. The operation became necessary because of problems with the movement of goods from Berlin across Soviet-controlled territory. Similarly, it was becoming impossible to supply the city with raw materials which in turn was playing a leading role in the economic recovery, so with the experience of the 1948-49 airlift, a similar operation was devised.

By mid-1952, both Surrey Flying Services and Fairflight had been absorbed into Air Charter which took up residence at Stansted. Ever since the Tudor had been inherited by the airline as part of the takeovers, Laker had been impressed by the performance of the type despite its chequered history. After prolonged negotiations, all the surviving stored specimens were acquired and transferred to Southend. Aviation Traders immediately embarked upon the comprehensive redesign work necessary, which eventually resulted in the award of an unrestricted certificate to carry passengers in February 1954.

This first rejuvenated Tudor entered service on Air Charter's coach class service between Stansted, Idris and Lagos, joined in due course by other modified machines. Some examples of the species were transformed into freighters with the addition of a large cargo door on the port side. In this guise the aircraft were known as Super Traders, performing very well on the airline's long haul charter services to the Pacific area, in addition to earning their keep on the lucrative German cargo runs.

Air Charter continued to employ the aircraft until 1959 when the type was retired for the second and final time. In the meantime, the airline had introduced the Douglas DC-4 in the mid-1950s, a type which not only undertook the same duties as the Super Traders, but which was to play a large part in the fortunes of the company at the end of the decade.

The Carvair offered great potential as a general freighter and it was this capability that was to take over as the car ferry business waned. G-AXAI entered service in April 1969 and served on until 1976.
via British World

CHANNEL AIR BRIDGE

Although heavily committed to contract work and its involvement with the Tudor, Air Charter decided to embark upon a completely new venture in 1954. Having noted the past success of Silver City's car ferry operations across the Channel, it was thought that a similar network with a departure point located north of the Thames would be popular with the travelling public and profitable for the company. Equipped with three of the short-nosed Freighter 31 variant, a short programme of trial services were flown five times per day between Southend and Calais from 1st September 1954. This development was viewed with some concern by Silver City because only a few weeks earlier it had opened the newly-built Lydd/Ferryfield, a bold step and one which needed considerable financial support. There were very real fears that a rival operation could dilute the market to such an extent that it would threaten the very existence of the airline.

After six weeks Air Charter suspended the services for the winter period as intended, using the time to review the performance and make any necessary changes to its plans. Although it was proposed to employ the existing Freighter 31s in the first instance, an order had been placed with the manufacturer for two examples of the Mk 32. The first of these was handed over at Bristol's Filton airfield on 25th March and by chance was the 200th example of the type produced. A month or so later it was joined by the 201st specimen, but by this time the ferry was underway following its launch on 4th April.

Frequency was fairly flexible and arranged to meet the anticipated demand, but for the first few weeks there were six daily returns, rising to 16 during May and finally 32 for the remainder of the peak season, before dropping back to 24 sor-

ties per day. Initially four of the company's Freighters flew the service, which was marketed as the Channel Air Bridge. The fifth aircraft was out-stationed in Germany for use on the Berlin to Hamburg and Hanover cargo runs.

The airline was not alone in having to adapt for this specialised business. It was necessary for Southend Airport to undertake some urgent work to cope with the influx of traffic, both from the air and road. This included laying a hard standing for the aircraft, the erection of a building for handling and Customs clearance, not to mention doubling the size of the terminal. Prior to this the facilities were only accustomed to irregular visits by DH Rapides and the like, so there was certainly a need for some expansion.

Departure arrangements followed the pattern established by Silver City, whereby the driver and passengers left the vehicle outside the terminal for one of the airline's staff to drive it to Customs and on to the aircraft. Once loading was complete, the car handler remained on board, transferring his attention to the needs of the passengers whilst airborne. Long after the end of the vehicle ferry services from Southend, the area devoted to the operation remained as a memorial to those hectic days of continuous activity.

Despite a poor first few months, the Channel Air Bridge soon started to expand, at the same time making money from the enterprise. A second route was introduced in October 1955 linking the airline's Essex base with Ostend. Not only was it a vehicle ferry, but in this case the company offered the service as a coach/air operation from London to Brussels. The success of the link did not go unnoticed by SABENA, the Belgian flag carrier, resulting in the two companies signing a pooling agreement in May 1957. As from 4th June the frequency of the service was set at six daily return sorties, but this total was doubled

during the summer peak. One Freighter 32 was repainted in SABENA's full livery but remained British registered. Several individual aircraft carried SABENA's colours during this time. Surface transport arrangements were modified so that non-motoring passengers travelled by train between London Liverpool Street and Southend, where preliminary steps were taken to construct a new station on the airport's perimeter. Sadly, this useful project never materialised.

Prior to the Belgian airline's involvement in Air Charter's ferry services, the latter had opened a Rotterdam schedule on 1st October 1956. Flown initially at a twice-daily frequency, the aircraft used the Dutch city's new airport at Zestienhoven, which still had no permanent buildings but was fully operational. It was built under extreme pressure from those of the opinion that one international airport is sufficient for a country of the Netherlands' size and this should be at Amsterdam. Nevertheless, since it was already the largest seaport in Europe, the city was determined that it would also have an airport capable of handling short haul international services. This ambition was certainly achieved, but Zestienhoven has remained relatively quiet, which probably supports the oppositions' viewpoint expressed 40 years ago.

Throughout this period Silver City continued to carry the bulk of the traffic, but its lead was steadily eroded. To make the operation more attractive and profitable it was essential that a more suitable type was introduced, especially since both operators were seriously considering the so-called 'deep penetration' routes once again. After each airline had submitted its list of European destinations to the licensing authority, the latter soon noted that there were a number of duplications. In a surprising demonstration of common sense by the Minister concerned, a pattern

of non-competitive services were allocated to each carrier in mid-1959.

One of the most important benefits to be gained was the higher annual utilisation figure for the aircraft. Since the short haul services were essentially seasonal, the Freighters only averaged about 1,000 hours per aircraft with the accompanying high operating costs. In the past Silver City had found it difficult to finance the acquisition of new equipment, a problem which did not affect Air Charter to the same extent.

During November 1958 talks began with the Airwork Group after the latter expressed an interest in taking over the airline. Indeed, it was not long before an agreement was reached which resulted in Air Charter becoming a subsidiary of the larger organisation in January 1959. Probably even more significant was the fact that the new owner decided that the ferry business should be divorced from the airline's other interests to operate as a completely separate company. Since the operation had been known as the Channel Air Bridge for some years, it seemed only logical to use this title for the new carrier which was subsequently created on 25th February.

THE CARVAIR

Fresh impetus was given to the task of selecting a Freighter replacement, but with the investigations largely centred upon finding an existing type suitable for conversion. The choice of Aviation Trader's chief designer, A C Leftley, was the Douglas DC-4, a type readily available in some numbers and consequently comparatively cheap with ample spares support. Having come to this conclusion, design work began immediately at the company's Southend facility on what was designated the ATL.98.

In order to meet the essential opening nose requirement, an entirely new forward fuselage was required. Various shapes and sizes were tested in the Cranfield wind tunnel, until finally a layout featuring an elevated flight deck almost 7ft higher than the original was chosen. To compensate for the additional side area produced by the bulbous nose section, a larger fin and rudder was provided, which transpired to be very similar to that carried on Douglas' DC-7 series. The ingeniously modified airliner was designed to carry up to five cars plus about 25 passengers in a cabin located at the rear of the fuselage, which was some 8ft 8in longer than that of the DC-4.

While these stages of the type's evolution were underway, Channel Air Bridge and Air Charter found themselves transferred to British United Airways, a new airline created by the merger of the Airwork and Hunting Clan, together with all their subsidiaries. The re-organised group officially began its operations on 1st July 1960. Fortunately, for the time being the car ferry operation was allowed to retain its name which therefore avoided the usual problem of informing customers of the change.

Meanwhile, the necessary approval had been received to proceed with the ATL.98, so the first aircraft earmarked for the conversion was moved into the Southend hangar. It proved to be Air Charter's G-ANYB, a former World Airways machine which had joined the company in 1955 to operate German services and trooping flights to Cyprus. The occasion was used to formally name the type, which henceforth was known as the Carvair. Chosen from a number of suggestions, it was derived from the words car-via-air, thereby reflecting the aircraft's future occupation.

Progress was sufficiently good to enable the prototype to be ready for the commencement of its flight trials on 21st June 1961. Its maiden trip aloft with D B Cartlidge at the controls proved uneventful, but the original estimate that a 60 hours programme would be sufficient to obtain its certificate was somewhat optimistic. Thereafter most of the test flying was carried out by Captain R Langley, until after some 155 hours in the air, the Carvair received its type certificate at the end of January 1962. Of course, sections of the airframe such as mainplanes and powerplant remained untouched and had accumulated over 37,000 hours as parts of the DC-4 before the major surgery had started.

The Carvair's first overseas flight took place on 16th February when the aircraft visited Ostend, but the inaugural scheduled service was operated by Channel Air Bridge on 1st March, with Rotterdam the chosen destination. Two more machines had rolled off the modification line before the start of the main summer season, and these proved extremely successful for the airline.

With the assistance of the Carvairs, the fleet carried over 300,000 passengers and 4,000 cars on the traditional short range flights, together with the recently introduced long haul sectors to Basle, Geneva and Strasbourg. The latter trio exceeded all expectations, but the results could have been even better had the capacity been available to handle the long waiting list of potential travellers.

Originally an Air Charter machine, Freighter G-APAU spent several years in SABENA livery to operate the Belgian carrier's car ferry services between Ostend and Southend. Taken at Southend, March 1961.
George Pennick

UNITED FRONT

Even before the start of the Carvair's flight trials, it was announced that the shareholders of British Aviation Services had accepted an approach by the Air Holdings Group. The latter had been created in November 1961 to act as a holding company for the proposed British United, of which Channel Air Bridge was already a subsidiary. It was apparent that the competition for the air ferry companies would come from the surface operators, as confidently forecast by those employed to produce such predictions. No longer were the shipping lines content to offer inadequate service, poor standards of comfort on board and a general shortage of capacity. There was now a vast improvement in the cross-Channel sea ferries, making the rivalry between the two airlines decidedly outdated. There was a growing need for all resources to be concentrated as effectively as possible, so under the circum-

stances the merger of Silver City and Channel Air Bridge was a wise, but unavoidable action. Although the move was announced in early 1962, it was 1st January 1963 before British United Air Ferries (BUAF) officially became operational.

Priority was given to the task of putting the new undertaking on a more economic basis resulting in higher tariffs together with a tighter control over capacity. Nevertheless, despite the caution and apprehension concerning the future, it was a time when the air ferry business was at its peak performance. After the spate of re-organisations earlier in the year, BUAF retained its main operating bases at Southend and Lydd, by which time the latter had dropped its Ferryfield title. From the south coast airport, Freighters continued to ply the routes to Ostend, Rotterdam and Le Touquet, the latter in association with the French carrier *Compagnie Air Transport*. The Carvair fleet was still small and remained at

When first converted by Aviation Traders in 1964, Aviaco operated this Carvair until bought by British United in 1965, at which point it was registered G-AOFW. In its DC-4 days it served with Pan American, Alitalia and Californian Eastern.
Mike Hooks

Southend, with two examples reconfigured to carry up to three cars and 55 passengers for use on the busy Ostend sector.

Extremely satisfying results were achieved during the 1963 summer programme with the 29-strong fleet carrying record loads on all services. The three long sector routes into France and Switzerland produced some impressive growth figures for the airline, which was sufficiently encouraged to expand its network of such services to include Liege in the following year. This was introduced from both Southend and Lydd with a Carvair operating from the Kent airport for the first time. Later that year the type was also used on the Jersey to Bournemouth route, while Freighters provided a regular link between Coventry and Calais from May, but this was to be one of the last sectors to be introduced by BUAF.

The long-expected decline began in 1964 when 109,000 cars were carried, a figure that two years later had fallen still further to 101,000, an ominous trend which would certainly continue. Additional modern ships were being relentlessly introduced on to the traditional crossings, while the service entry of the hovercraft also played its part in attracting many of the carrier's previous customers. Carrying 30 cars and passengers, this latest mode of transport offered airliner type accommodation complete with cabin attendants for the swift journeys. These were known as flights rather than sailings, while the driver became a pilot. It gave the defectors from the air ferries a familiar atmosphere even if the crossing was at a much lower altitude than before!

Bearing in mind the popularity of the longer sectors only two or three years earlier, the rapid change in the level of support in 1966 was most disappointing. A number of measures had been taken to bring a halt to the growing loss of business including a 15% cut in fares on the short cross-Channel routes and a greater emphasis on freight traffic. Despite this action, the services still lost money during the year and all the signs indicated that 1967 would not bring any improvement. The airline was therefore faced with the need to re-organise and consolidate its operations immediately, otherwise it would find it difficult to continue after the end of the year.

Steps were taken in February 1967 to suspend all of the 'deep penetration' flights together with other unprofitable services. These included the flights from British regional airports such as Manchester and Coventry, plus several from both Southend and Lydd. The Essex airport handled its final regular Freighter movement on 31st March when the incoming flight from Calais arrived for the last time after almost 13 years of operation. Any future appearances of the type were normally for maintenance purposes, charters or to provide relief for overbooked Carvairs.

The pruning exercise continued during the following September when the airline ended services that linked Southampton to the Channel Islands and Cherbourg. Although a popular operation, the routes were too seasonal to remain viable. Such cutbacks brought a reduction in fleet size, resulting in a number of aircraft being stored or scrapped. The latter fate befell several Freighters that were near the end of their spar lives anyway.

Studies were carried out to find a way to reverse the company's downward spiral, concluding that it would probably return to profitability if given greater freedom. For the past five years or so the BUAF identity was used to reflect the close association with BUA within the Air Holdings group. This was no longer necessary, so the suggested separation was agreed by the Board on 1st October 1967, a date which marked the creation of British Air Ferries (BAF).

Providing runway 06 was in use at Southend, the low level approaches of the Carvairs always provided interesting shots. G-APNH 'Menai Bridge' on finals.
Author

A familiar scene at Lydd in days gone by. Freighter Mk 32 G-ANVR carrying the new BAF livery while its companion on the apron (G-APAU) retains that of British United. But both car ramps have received the new logos!
Author

No time was lost in becoming a self-contained unit, with the main objective being to cut costs. This was largely achieved by a 25% reduction in staff, but other substantial savings were possible by moving the central reservations organisation from London to Southend. Similarly, the expensive accommodation occupied in Victoria was released by the airline in favour of offices located at its Essex operating base. Some months after BAF was conceived, a number of Air Holdings' aviation interests were sold, including BUA and its subsidiary companies. Somewhat significantly the transaction did not include BAF or Aviation Traders, both remaining with Air Holdings.

The trimmed down airline started 1968 with renewed confidence, operating a fleet of five Carvairs on routes from Southend to Calais, Ostend and Rotterdam, with a similar number of Freighters serving Deauville, Le Touquet and Ostend from Lydd. Traffic showed signs of a revival in the early months, much of it due to the new sales department and increased marketing efforts. Such activities had previously been handled by BUA, but the wide variation between the types of operation of the two carriers made the arrangement less than satisfactory. Unfortunately, most of the advances made during the early months of the year were lost through circumstances beyond BAF's control. A general strike in France caused numerous cancellations of services for six weeks in May and June, the cost to the airline being over £60,000 in lost revenue. As if this was not enough, an outbreak of foot and mouth disease in Britain badly affected the meat and livestock charter traffic using Lydd.

The latter airport was already becoming much quieter following the general reduction of services, so BAF began exploring ideas to boost the under-used facility. One such enterprise involved the use of a light hovercraft to give joyrides over a course laid out on the grass, an attraction aimed particularly at the customers of the nearby holiday camps. This venture was deemed responsible for the marked increase in car park, bar and restaurant takings which all helped to swell the depleted coffers!

The airport's aviation connections were not forgotten because steps were taken to encourage greater use by general aviation and private flyers leaving or entering the country. In the longer term, BAF also had an outline plan to develop Lydd as a hoverport for cross-Channel operations. Although not actually on the coast, it was considered a relatively simple undertaking to provide a water-filled channel across the flat terrain between the airport and the sea. This form of access would produce far less wear and tear to the hovercrafts' skirts than would be the case if travelling over land. Two potential operators were approached with the project but decided against the site, choosing instead to use Pegwell Bay and Dover. Needless to say the scheme was dropped at an early stage leaving Lydd to handle the dwindling car ferry flights.

It had always been acknowledged that the success of the vehicle services depended on achieving the correct balance between cars, passengers and freight. This was possible to some extent with the Carvair, which was sufficiently flexible to cope with the changing loads. On average it could be reconfigured from a five car and 22 passengers layout to accommodate 55 passengers plus two or three cars, depending on size, in about 40 minutes. The Southend flights to Rotterdam and Ostend were already popular as a cheaper alternative to flying from London to the Continent, with the Belgian airport also providing the connection for the Brussels rail link.

Vehicle fares charged by BAF were now higher than those of the sea ferries, but the airline considered that the level was the lowest that could be sensibly offered. On the other hand increases were avoided if at all possible, otherwise it was feared yet more travellers would desert the air ferries.

The extent of this defection became apparent when BAF announced that it was now carrying some 5% of the total vehicle traffic to mainland Europe, compared with the peak performance of 27% only a few years earlier. Fortunately, the lower figure had stabilised and represented the motorists who were prepared to pay a little more in exchange for a speedier service with individual attention, a market which showed signs of growth according to the travel industry. Additional freight contracts were also forthcoming to generally increase the carrier's involvement in this type of business together with the aircraft's utilisation figures.

While relieved that the immediate danger had passed, BAF realised that one of the main problems that had to be tackled in the near future was the replacement of the surviving five Freighters. Although possible to undertake modifications to extend their spar lives, in view of the deteriorating vehicle business the expense hardly seemed justified. If necessary the Carvair could take over the Lydd duties, but the machine was really not ideal for the short

sectors flown. There appeared to be no easy solution. In the event the Freighters out lived the service they provided, because at the end of October 1970 one of the fleet operated the final return ferry run between Lydd and Le Touquet. The Carvair operated Ostend schedule was still offered, but this link was also severed early in the next year.

Under the circumstances there was little the company could do but to accept the inevitable. Trial operations had already begun in the spring of 1970 with an all-passenger Viscount leased from Aer Lingus. It became BAF's first turboprop

aircraft and was used to maintain some of the scheduled services to Ostend and Le Touquet from Southend. The aircraft proved very successful and stayed with the carrier until October 1971, having been joined in its second year by a pair of Court Line Hawker Siddeley HS.748s. But as the trio returned to their respective owners at the end of the summer season, news of an ownership change was released by BAF. Control of the company had passed from Air Holdings to T D (Mike) Keegan, already a major shareholder in Stansted-based Trans Meridian Air Cargo which he had founded in 1962.

By October 1968 Carvair G-ASDC had acquired BAF titles but otherwise the livery remained unchanged. On this occasion the aircraft was using Stansted for some 'engine out' approaches.
George Pennick

Car Ferry Finale

Throughout October 1971 there had been growing speculation about the future of BAF. Although there was no comment from the airline, it was widely reported that the remaining Carvairs were to be withdrawn and replaced with Canadair CL-44s, the type operated by Trans Meridian Air Cargo (TMAC). Further credence was given when the latter advertised for ten crews to meet its staffing requirements after increasing the fleet size to nine aircraft. On 27th October all was revealed, but it was something of an anti-climax because most of the rumours were found to be true!

Mike Keegan was well known at Southend after his association with Crewsair, Crewsair Engineering and BKS Air Transport, companies he had played a large part in creating after leaving the RAF as a Flight Sergeant. Few doubted that there would be changes and no one was disappointed. Hitherto the airline had been controlled by a rarely-seen board of directors, so the frequent appearance of the knowledgeable new chairman introduced a more personal touch, with most of the staff known by Christian name.

Although approachable and always willing to help anyone with problems, he remained a strict disciplinarian and would not countenance malingering. Extended meal breaks were not favoured and it is said that he sacked a person observed munching sandwiches outside the specified period, only to learn that the individual was not employed by BAF anyway!

Soon after the take over of the company, a policy statement was issued which confirmed that the five active Carvairs would be retired within six months, resulting in 38 staff losing their jobs, one member being Captain R Langley, the company's long-serving chief pilot. At the same time Southend Council, as owner of the airport, received a strongly-worded letter to the effect that if no action was taken to extend the main runway 06/24 from 5,500ft to 6,000ft within six months, the entire BAF operation would be moved to Stansted.

Councils as a breed are not renowned for swift action, so there was little chance of success with this demand and certainly not within the time scale requested. In any case, it was not the first time that the subject had been raised through the years, but feasibility studies had always ruled out the development. Nothing had changed in the meantime, so the same difficult problem remained. Any extension would mean diverting a public road, the demolition of some buildings and an increase in noise, something the local authorities could not accept even if it meant losing the business of one of its largest operators.

Southend Council probably guessed that when the airline realised the implications of the proposed action, it would modify its plans accordingly. Landing fees at Southend were reduced for BAF's aircraft operating the Le Touquet and Ostend services, a concession not available at Stansted.

Also, Stansted did not possess a dedicated building capable of handling the volume of freight involved, neither could the passenger terminal building cope with an influx of an additional 250,000 travellers per year. It was already proving inadequate for the ITs and schedules of Channel Airways, so it was in BAF's best interest to avoid the bad publicity resulting from the over crowding.

As suspected, BAF decided against the move, although the plan to introduce the CL-44 on to

The last of the initial Herald trio to be delivered to BAF was G-BDFE. This was converted into a VIP aircraft with a capacity of 23 seats in first class configuration, but later it was restored to normal airline use for leasing to various customers.
via British World

The CL-44 G-AZIN was the first of two to be repainted in BAF livery in the Spring of 1972. Its career with the airline was short and quickly reverted to its original role with Stansted-based Transmeridian Air Cargo.
Author

vehicle services from Stansted to Basle and Ostend continued. It seemed a strange decision at a time when both the long and short haul ferries had already become distinctly unprofitable due to lack of interest by the travelling public. Regardless of this fact, the carrier announced plans to have a fleet of eight aircraft by February 1972, two equipped with 75 seats and the capacity for five cars and cargo, one with a high-density 175-seat layout for use on IT work, while four would remain freighters but with the ability for rapid conversion for passenger services when necessary. The eighth was earmarked for special duties concerned with a series of proposed air cruises to the Caribbean, Africa and the Far East. A high standard of comfort was to be achieved by limiting the capacity to 100 seats for the luxury excursions, with other attractions including a cocktail bar, gaming tables and a roulette wheel.

In readiness for the new venture, a CL-44 was transferred from TMAC for overhaul and the installation of its passenger interior at Southend. Three days after roll out on 25th March 1972, the aircraft uplifted 170 passengers and nine crew bound for Ostend, at the time the largest load ever carried from the airport. Flights from Stansted to the Belgian airport began over the Easter period at a basic frequency of twice-daily, but during the summer it was intended to operate five return trips per day with the CL-44 in passenger configuration. With the delivery of the second machine in mid-May, BAF was able to launch the vehicle ferry sorties thereby increasing the total daily flights to nine.

It was confidently expected that this would generate some 230,000 passengers annually, but after only a week or two, poor loads disproved this estimate. Without more ado the operation was swiftly ended, followed in July by the return of both aircraft to TMAC prior to resuming their careers as freighters. The type's sojourn with BAF was therefore short, but this was not entirely surprising since it was hardly ideal for the role. Although perfectly capable of carrying 175 passengers over 3,500 miles, the CL-44 was not at all happy with the 35 minute sector to Ostend. Neither was it easy for the four cabin attendants because no sooner had they completed the departure formalities, than it was time to start the disembarking process. This needed to be carried out speedily if the essential short turn-arounds were to be accomplished, but in practice it proved very difficult. Opening the swing tail could have hastened exit, but this was sealed on the passenger machine.

As a consequence of this change of plan it was necessary to sub charter a variety of aircraft from other carriers to meet the commitments, but at the same time a start was made on a Carvair modification programme. This included the complete refurbishment of the passenger cabin which had previously contained somewhat basic accommodation. Every effort was made to improve the image by producing a bright new decor for the interior, while the occupants enjoyed greater comfort by reducing the number of seats installed. Of course, the aft position of the cabin remained unchanged by necessity, so did its tendency to reflect the movements of the aircraft as it trundled along. Total capacity remained variable because the bulkhead separating the compartment from the freight hold could be moved as required, thereby giving greater flexibility for varying the mix of cars, freight and passengers. Each Carvair was given a smart two-tone blue livery and a name in recognition of its out-sized appearance. Hence *Porky Pete*, *Fat Albert* and *Big John* were amongst those to be seen.

Despite having more Carvairs available, there was still a requirement for more capacity during the 1973 season. This time East Midlands-based Alidair provided a Viscount, which, for the duration of its stay at Southend, was mainly employed on BAF's schedules to Ostend. During the year it was also planned to resurrect several services from Coventry, but a series of problems caused the scheme to be abandoned. The reasons were outlined in a strongly-worded statement by BAF's chairman who blamed industrial action by airport staff, a complete lack of passenger facilities even to the extent of providing a modest snack bar service at convenient times, together with an apparent disinterest on the part of the management. The cumulative effect rendered the operation of scheduled services from Coventry quite impractical, although outstanding commitments were honoured to avoid disappointment to the public and cargo shippers. At this stage BAF was recording an average of 87% for on-time departures at Southend, with over 90% of the flights leaving within 15 minutes. Less than half these figures were reached at Coventry, which was an unacceptable performance and could not be tolerated.

Until 1973 it had always been the custom to contract most of any refurbishments, major overhauls and routine maintenance to Aviation Traders. In the middle of the year BAF announced that it intended to establish its own engineering base at Southend by taking over two of the hangars previously used by the now-defunct Channel Airways. Modifications were carried out to the doors to allow the entry of the Carvair's high nose prior to the facility's opening at the end of August when some 100 engineers had been recruited. The modern complex became operational at the end of the year with the projected staff level expected to be doubled.

The unit also established an organisation known as Hawke Aircraft Parts for the manufacture and repair of components, while a glass fibre division possessed the technical skills to cater for all sections of industry. In due course the company became involved in car racing by producing its own Formula Ford vehicle. Known as the BAF Special, the car was driven by the chairman's son, Rupert Keegan, and was considered an ideal way to promote the car ferry services. Airline personnel were encouraged to form a fan club, with members frequently flown to the various venues in the company's DC-3, which, needless to say, was piloted by Mike Keegan.

Another product of the versatile company was the ultimate in motor homes. The converted coach's luxuriously appointed interior was divided into two compartments, both equipped with air conditioning and heating. The rear half could seat up to ten travellers, while the forward section accommodated the kitchen facilities which included all essential items such as freezer, microwave, electric and gas cooker, all powered by the vehicle's own generator. Named the BAF Land Yacht, it could be produced for use in a number of different roles ranging from a mobile hospital, office and conference room, or as a VIP transport with limited seating. In the event only one was completed and was used by BAF to attend European Formula One meetings.

Meanwhile, BAF continued its attempts to revive the air ferry market with the introduction of new or re-instated routes into Europe, but none survived for very long. This forced the airline to recognise the fact that the once-popular method of moving vehicles to mainland Europe was no longer viable. Undoubtedly, if the company was to remain in business there had to be an expansion of services using a more suitable type of airliner than the lumbering Carvairs. Moreover, despite the rejuvenation of the latter, the hardworking aircraft were beginning to suffer from more than an acceptable level of unserviceability. Unselfishly, the aircraft's four Pratt & Whitney engines began to share some of their oil with those living under or near the flight paths of the airports visited. This in turn led to a growing number of complaints about ruined washing, which hardly endeared the type or airline to the affected residents. So while the Carvairs continued with various freight charters and the remaining ferry and passenger schedules, the airline considered which type would be suitable for the route network flown.

A NEW ERA HERALDED

It was the Handley Page Herald which was finally chosen, three being purchased from the Canadian carrier, Eastern Provincial Airways. The first specimen was flown to Southend in late January 1975 to begin route proving within a few days. It was joined by the second example of the breed

Between 1971 and 1974 the DC-3 G-AJRY was used as a company VIP transport, frequently attending motor race meetings in connection with BAF's involvement in the sport. It carried the inscription 'Executive Jet' on the nose together with Transmeridian's crest.
Author

BAF was also involved with motor racing in the 1970s when it sponsored a Formula Ford car. Driver of the BAF Special Royale was the Chairman's son, Rupert Keegan.
via British World

BAF's Heralds were to be seen in many different liveries, Trans Azur Aviation being the future operator of G-BDZV in 1981.
Author

during March, to operate the first revenue earning flight on 17th April. Unfortunately, the remaining member of the trio was severely bent in a wheels-up landing just before its delivery flight. At one point it was thought that it was beyond repair, but after an inspection by BAF's engineers and some ingenious temporary repairs, the Herald reached Southend in early July. After a lengthy overhaul, it finally entered service in December configured with a quick-change cabin that offered either 50 seats or executive style accommodation for 21 passengers.

The year ended with the Group's financial report which revealed that of the £1.25 million profit, BAF's contribution was £250,000 while BAF Engineering only managed £50,000. The bulk was therefore produced by TMAC, but this was understandable bearing in mind that BAF had higher depreciation costs on its Heralds and also looked after the cargo carrier's administration needs.

Although BAF still had four Carvairs in service, since the support for the car ferries had reached an all-time low point, the airline proposed to allocate only one aircraft to these duties in 1976, leaving the remaining three for freight work. This meant that more replacements were needed, especially since several leasing contracts had been acquired for the existing Heralds.

Although a popular and reliable type, the Herald did not enjoy the success it deserved with only 48 examples completed at the time of the manufacturer's demise in 1970. Second-hand examples were therefore not plentiful, but BAF managed to locate three in South America where they had been operated by Transbrasil. The first of the newcomers arrived at Southend at the end of June, entering commercial service at Southend on 18th July. All three had been delivered by the end of August, one being the shorter, pre-production variant which differed considerably from the standard machine. Because its lack of commonality, it was expected that Series 100 G-APWA would end its days as a spares source for its more fortunate colleagues, but surprisingly this was not the case. In due course it was overhauled to spend several profitable years on lease.

Having survived a fairly lean period, BAF began to consider the expansion of its scheduled services. One such addition was the Calais route which was re-instated in the network after being dropped in 1972 due to the declining traffic. With the growing number of business travellers crossing the Channel, all the indications pointed to a successful relaunch. In this case the market re-

search appears to have been misleading, because the expected Herald loads of passengers were missing. Instead there were barely sufficient to fill a nine-seat DH Dove, which substituted for the larger airliner until the service was permanently abandoned. Other sectors proposed included Lille, Dusseldorf, Antwerp, Rotterdam, Hanover and Luxembourg. In order to meet these commitments the search continued for more Heralds. This time two were found nearer home, with British Midland, so delivery in January 1977 only involved a short journey from East Midlands.

An occasion worthy of greater attention was the final car ferry flight by a BAF Carvair on New Year's Day, the last of innumerable sorties since the enterprise began back in 1948. Such was the decline in demand for these services that this activity had accounted for only 5% of BAF's business in 1976. Nevertheless, there was still plenty of work for the remaining aircraft, which continued to roam far and wide with freight charters.

In late June BAF severed its connection with TMAC when the latter was sold by the Keegan Group for £3.37million. The new owner was the Cunard Shipping Company which acquired the cargo carrier at a time when it was replacing its CL-44s with Douglas DC-8 jets and was making a profit.

This transaction coincided with a report that BAF had acquired the entire fleet of Heralds operated by the Royal Malaysian Air Force (RMAF), although it hardly seemed likely that the deal would be completed. On the other hand, the airline had a growing number of promising lease contracts in the offing, so it was anxious to add to its fleet which now contained eight assorted specimens. Any doubts disappeared when the first of the demobbed Heralds flew into Southend on 15th August after its lengthy journey back to its homeland. This military version was known as the Series 400 and differed from the standard Series 200 by possessing a strengthened floor and rearward-facing seats. Eight aircraft had been delivered in 1964 and all were included in the purchase, although one of the batch had suffered an accident while still in RMAF service. After inspection, BAF decided that it would be uneconomic to restore it to flying condition so it was eventually reduced to spares at Kuala Lumpur. The remaining seven were delivered at regular intervals spread over a number of months, whereupon they were overhauled and given BAF's blue and yellow livery before entering service. The work involved the provision of a completely new

cabin interior, together with modifications to bulkheads and galley equipment. All of this was completed by BAF Engineering in a commendably short time, enabling the first Series 400 to begin its civilian career on 6th October with the schedule to Rotterdam.

Now possessing a fleet of 15 Heralds, BAF was able to meet specialist requirements by converting one of the ex-Canadian Series 200s (G-BDFE) into a VIP transport complete with eight side couches in the boardroom area, an eight-track sound and cassette system and video equipment. First class meals and bar service were served throughout the flight, the cost being included in the charter price. During 1978 the engineering division also converted one of the ex Malaysian machines for all-cargo work. The stripped interior allowed the payload to increase considerably to 13,046lb (5,918kg).

There were seldom times when rumours did not circulate around the Southend base about future plans for the airline. In 1978 the principal

tale related to the end of scheduled services in order to concentrate on the more lucrative and less demanding leasing and charter business or even the sale of the aircraft if the price was right. Eventually a statement was issued by British Island Airways (BIA) that an agreement had been reached whereby it would be taking over all of BAF's schedules with effect from 1st January 1979. Although already operating the Herald in some numbers, BIA certainly did not have sufficient capacity to cover the additional services. As a result the deal included the lease of six examples of the type from BAF, the latter remaining responsible for engineering back-up. It also meant that 140 members of staff were transferred to BIA, leaving about 40 from the clerical and reservations departments to face redundancy.

Had more Heralds been readily available, then no doubt the Keegan Group would have added them to the fleet, since leasing opportunities continued to present themselves. Most of the remaining members of the fleet were flown in the unfamiliar liveries of far-flung customers for long term contracts, while those spending short spells with other carriers displayed temporary titles but were not repainted. From BAF's point of view, the expanding business indicated the need for an alternative type, preferably offering greater capacity. It was a convenient point to ponder on such things because British Airways was about to retire its large fleet of Viscounts, thereby providing an ideal opportunity to acquire some well maintained and inexpensive aircraft.

ENTER THE VISCOUNT

Negotiations were successfully completed with the national carrier during 1980, resulting in the purchase of six examples of the popular airliner. Although some had been in store at Cardiff since the spring, regular maintenance had continued throughout this period. This included the careful sealing of vulnerable parts and regular engine runs to ensure there was no deterioration. The first of the batch was flown to Southend on 16th January 1981 to undergo a thorough overhaul with BAF Engineering before its official unveiling on 4th February, almost 24 years after its first flight.

Its appearance certainly belied its age because blue, white and yellow bands had been applied to the basic BA livery on the fuselage and fin, while the fight deck roof had been repainted yellow. Internally, the decor produced an attractive appearance with bright new covers for the 76 seats. The subsequent presentation to the press and travel trade was mainly to explain the reason for the company re-entering the IT market with a turboprop when jets were in common use for such flights. By using the Viscount it was possible to offer tour operators a comfortable and reliable aircraft with seat mile costs that were substantially lower than those of the BAC One-Eleven, HS Trident or Fokker Fellowship. It was also confidently forecast that in the following year the DC-8, Boeing 720 and 707 would be added to this list. To illustrate the point, figures were provided for flights to a number of popular destinations including short range sectors to Amsterdam, Brussels and Ostend and longer range sorties to Rimini, Madrid and Barcelona.

Attention was also drawn to the presence of an HS.125, one of two acquired by BAF for use as eight-seat executive transports. Alternatively the aircraft could be converted in about two hours to carry a stretcher, medical equipment and nursing staff, a useful facility which kept the twin-jets gainfully employed.

During the course of 1981 BAF's Viscount collection began to grow rapidly. More examples were purchased from BA in March, followed by the flag carrier's remaining seven as they were retired at the end of the year. Unlike the earlier aircraft, the final machines were delivered immediately after the completion of a scheduled service, arriving at Southend or Cardiff in full BA livery. By this time BAF Engineering had already taken over the maintenance of the type at Cardiff's Rhoose Airport and was preparing to develop the facility in association with the existing unit at its Essex base. Another subsidiary, Dragon Light Aircraft, was formed at Cardiff to develop a small microlight aircraft. The programme did not advance far and after a series of problems the project was quietly dropped. This occurred just before the Keegan Group made the decision to concentrate its resources on its leasing and engineering divisions.

Meanwhile, BAF had also bought one of the longer range Viscount 810 variants in order to operate regular charters to Palma and Malaga. Fortunately, Southend Council had finally approved an outlay of £550,000 to remove the obstructions at the end of runway 24. These had seriously affected the Herald's payload, particularly in high summer temperatures. By the spring of 1981 all of the various sheds and cottages had been demolished, an earth bank reduced in height and traffic lights installed to prevent the possible conversion of passing double-deck buses to open-top configuration!

Barely six months after the first Viscount was delivered to Southend, BAF announced that it expected to acquire at least ten British Aerospace (BAe) 146s four-engined jetliners over the next two years. This statement was no doubt welcomed by BAe since it came at a time when the type had just been rolled out at Hatfield and was about to start its lengthy test programme. It was the airline's intention to employ four of the 80-seat aircraft for charter work, thereby replacing the 76-seat Viscounts for these duties.

No order was forthcoming from the company, but just over a year later applications were submitted to the Civil Aviation Authority (CAA) for licences to operate scheduled services from Heathrow to Innsbruck, Cannes, St Moritz (Samedan) and Lourdes (Tarbes), the 146 being the only jet airliner capable of flying into those airports at that time. No doubt BAF's apparent interest in the type influenced BAe when selecting a carrier to undertake the

In April 1982 Air Manchester began operating One-Eleven 416 G-AVOE for Sureways Travel. Appropriately re-registered G-SURE, after a difficult summer programme, the company decided to move its end-of-season charters from Manchester to Liverpool, at the same time contracting BAF to operate the flights. Accordingly the aircraft was repainted but the venture ended in November when the aircraft returned to British Aerospace.
via British World

commercial route proving flights prior to the issue of the type certificate. Consequently, the fourth airframe was painted in the airline's full livery complete with the appropriate registration G-OBAF. Following an appearance at that year's Farnborough Show, the intensive series began in December 1982 with the 21 days schedule interrupted only by Christmas.

All sorties had to be made by regular airline crews with the conditions fully representative of normal operations. Observers from the CAA were carried on all flights which were completed in 175 hours over 151 sectors, with various airports used as the departure points to overseas destinations such as Munich, Dusseldorf, Beauvais and Toulouse. Fuel efficiency proved to be some 6% better than had been anticipated, while domestic turn-around times were impressively speedy.

From this practical experience, BAF was convinced that the 146 was ideal for its long-term leasing business in hot and high conditions, so it

began talks with possible customers. Surprisingly, despite the interest shown by a number of UK tour operators, there was insufficient support to keep an aircraft fully employed on European charter work. In the event another eight years passed before the airline began to operate the 146 commercially for IT charters.

This series of trials was not BAF's first encounter with jet airliners, because during the summer of 1982 the airline operated a One-Eleven 400 for Pennine Commercial Holdings, the parent company of Air Manchester. Sureway Travel had decided to create its own in-house airline to carry its clients to the European sunspots, but due to a distinct lack of experience it was only a short time before it decided to contract the flying to an established company. BAF took over the duties and the sole aircraft employed was repainted to reflect the change. At the end of the season the One-Eleven was returned to the manufacturer and BAF's brief encounter with the type ended until the end of the decade.

Scheduled Growth

During 1982 it became known that BAF intended to opt out of commercial flying by selling this element of the business. In the following March this was achieved, the new owner being Jadepoint, a London-based company associated with property development and Grants Department Store in Croydon rather than the aviation industry. Some £2 million was paid for the carrier, with the transaction including only five Viscounts and two Heralds. The remaining members of the fleet, BAF Engineering and the company's title were not included in the sale because Keegan intended to continue with the leasing and maintenance divisions. As a consequence, a new identity was needed for the airline, so it was decided to transfer a name previously used by the leisure division. This was BAF Air Tours, but before it could be applied to the aircraft, the Keegan Group somewhat unexpectedly ceased trading. Jadepoint was therefore able to acquire the remainder of the fleet, the title and the engineering company, the latter becoming Jadepoint Aircraft Engineering. In addition, all contracts held with various tour operators were transferred, together with the travel outlets Viscount Holidays and Viscount Travel.

At the time of the sale, BAF's main business involved ITs to the Channel Islands and scheduled freight services to Dusseldorf, Basle and Belfast. Both the chairman and managing director, Robin Pesskin and Alan Weiner respectively, expressed the view that the change of ownership would greatly assist the development of the company's operations. There was certainly a different technique used by the new management compared with the firm control of the shrewd Mike Keegan, but the new regime brought a fresh approach and had the full support of the staff. So with all the aircraft fully committed for the summer season and with Jadepoint's strong backing, it was felt that the basis was established for steady growth in the coming years.

One of the first signs of expansion came in April when BAF announced the opening of a Channel Islands' base and the formation of Jersey Air Ferries (JAF). Two Viscounts were earmarked for transfer to this subsidiary carrier, which intended to provide extensive summer charter services to Jersey for a number of tour operators including Ile Verte, Travtel, Gala Holidays, Jubilee, Bellingham and Travel Care. Bearing in mind that the island provided a major market for BAF, the step was considered logical and demonstrated the company's total commitment to the provision of a large charter facility for both business and leisure traffic.

The first aircraft appeared at Southend on 27th April 1983 resplendent in an attractive colour scheme and JAF titles prior to positioning to its new base. Upon arrival a naming ritual was performed by the current Miss Battle of Flowers before the aircraft set off on its inaugural service to Le Touquet. While charters provided the immediate employment for the Viscount, it was planned that future expansion would include a number of scheduled services. This was confirmed at an early stage when the first licence application was submitted to the CAA for authority to operate between Jersey and Manston on a regular basis. Throughout the summer the solitary Viscount was kept busy, but despite the promotional publicity afforded the project, by October JAF had been quietly dropped and the aircraft repainted in BAF livery.

In the meantime Jadepoint had added another

Jersey Air Ferries was launched in April 1983 for operations from the Channel Islands, but the project was ended in October whereupon the airline's sole Viscount (G-AOYP) was returned to BAF. It was still in service in 1996 but now registered G-PFBT for duties with Parcel Force.
Author

company to its group, namely Guernsey Airlines. The carrier had been formed in April 1978 as a subsidiary of Alidair, an East Midlands-based company, to provide both charter and scheduled services. When British Airways announced in 1979 that it proposed to drop 26 routes from its network, many involved the Channel Islands, particularly Guernsey. Needless to say, Guernsey Airlines was one of a number of independent carriers which promptly applied for the routes serving its home island from Southampton, Gatwick, Heathrow and Manchester. Unfortunately, its only success was the Manchester sector which was insufficient to justify additional equipment. A solitary Viscount leased from its parent company was employed on the schedule in 1981, but in the following year the company took over the Cambridge and Staverton routes, adding a Shorts 330 for the purpose, again leased from Alidair. Seasonal routes included those between Guernsey, Prestwick and Newcastle.

In September 1982 the company achieved a notable success when it was awarded the Gatwick-Guernsey route by the CAA at the expense of Air UK. The latter had been awarded the licence when it was relinquished by British Airways two years earlier, but it had attracted a fair amount of criticism for the general condition of its Heralds. Surprisingly, the change from the pressurised type to the smaller unpressurised '330 met with little public resistance when Guernsey Airlines took over on 1st April 1983. In fact, passengers were pleasantly surprised at the amount of room available. Air UK appealed in vain using the over-the-weather ability as a major feature of the case, but the islanders actually wanted their own airline and now at last they had it operating on one of the main life lines with London.

Unfortunately, while Guernsey Airlines was experiencing some success, its parent – now known as Inter City Airlines – was struggling to survive. Its efforts came to an end on 1st August, when the airline was put into the hands of the Receiver shortly after selling its subsidiary to the expanding Jadepoint. This acquisition was a far more ambitious undertaking for the latter company because existing scheduled services were

When BAF purchased Guernsey Airlines in 1983, Herald G-ASVO was transferred to give additional capacity on the busy London route. The aircraft retained the parent's livery but was given Guernsey Airlines titles. 'Victor Oscar' on finals for Gatwick, September 1983.
George Pennick

Shorts 330 G-BITX was one of several examples of the type employed by Guernsey Airlines for its Channel Islands' scheduled services. In this case the aircraft was on strength between December 1983 and September 1987 before being sold.
Author

involved, particularly the newly-won Gatwick route. The '330 normally employed was included in the sale, but the new owner declined the offer of the Viscount because it was a Series 700 aircraft and therefore incompatible with the BAF fleet.

Jadepoint also inherited the valuable Shell oil charter contracts in Scotland, which specified four daily round trips between Aberdeen and Sumburgh. These accounted for the movement of some 5,500 passengers per month plus about 55,100lb of cargo, many of the sorties being flown in extremely difficult weather conditions. Two Viscount 800s were stationed at Aberdeen, one being a standby aircraft to ensure maximum reliability in the event of unserviceability of its companion, such was the importance of the contract.

Almost immediately one of BAF's Heralds was given Guernsey titles and pressed into service when necessary, particularly on the weekend London flights. Jadepoint formally explained

the latest arrangements and its future plans on 18th August when a Viscount 800 was transferred to the company by BAF. At the same time any fears that the local residents might have had about the future of Guernsey Airlines were allayed by the new management. It was emphasised that there was no intention of changing its name to British Air Ferries or even Guernsey Air Ferries, the main aim being to strengthen the airline and give it the advantages of a flexible fleet. The occasion was also used to announce that an agreement had been signed with British Caledonian for better interlining at Gatwick, together with closer liaison with the travel trade.

Any lingering doubts amongst the islanders were effectively dispelled by the airline's performance during the following months, when frequencies were steadily improved. It was a happy state of affairs for the Guernsey population who now had a reliable carrier with a promising future. From Jadepoint's viewpoint, its two airlines were producing good returns on the investment, thereby confirming that the company had made the right decision when it became involved in this industry.

Towards the end of the year the company launched its latest scheme known as the 'Skyrider', which was designed to meet the revival of coach/air tours. In noting this trend, BAF signed a £3 million contract with National Holidays whereby the coach company transferred its clients to Southend in readiness for the 22 minute flight to Ostend. Onward transportation was provided by continental companies usually employing modern 76-seat double-deck coaches equipped with air conditioning, video entertainment, galley and toilet facilities.

BAF's commercial director, Mike Kay, was enthusiastic about the project, which eliminated the need for British coach operators to take their vehicles to the continent, thereby saving money on the sea crossing and the wear and tear on the long European journeys to the various resorts. Those heading for the Spanish Costa Brava had the daunting prospect of a 20-hour trip ahead of them, at the end of which even the most hardy of passengers had begun to wilt. Nevertheless, for those otherwise unable to afford a foreign break, the programme provided a relatively cheap holiday on the Mediterranean coast or alternatively a similar excursion to the Austrian mountain districts. In addition, both Southend-based Viscount Holidays and Viscount Travel were offering a wider range of ITs both on mainland Europe and the Channel Islands.

NETWORK EXPANSION

In the meantime, the BAF Group's scheduled service network was also beginning to expand. The company had gained a good base for growth when it acquired the established Gatwick-Guernsey route which quickly offered a minimum of four daily return services. Direct services were added from numerous regional airports until the Channel Islands were linked with Aberdeen, Cambridge, Edinburgh, Glasgow, Humberside, Manchester, Manston, Newcastle, Southend and Tees-side. Throughout 1984-85 both BAF and Guernsey Airlines continued to enjoy considerable success, the Channel Islands playing a significant part in the company's profitability. Such was the demand that over the weekend of 20th/21st July 1985, the two airlines operated 178 flights to Jersey and Guernsey, representing a 38% increase on the same period a year earlier. Although the available combined fleet totalled 18 aircraft at this point, it even became necessary to charter additional capacity from other British carriers.

Not surprisingly, BAF was now the world's largest operator of the Viscount which was chiefly responsible for the company's impressive performance. Indeed, the management was convinced that there was no other aircraft on the British civil register that could compare in terms of capital costs, operating costs and payload. It was also very popular with the passengers who appreciated the comfortable and roomy interior, while magnificent views were possible through the large old-style oval windows. With these factors in mind, BAF sought to extend the veterans' life from the 30 years arbitrarily fixed at the time of manufacture, to 45 years or 75,000 landings, whichever came first. A programme was agreed in conjunction with BAe whereupon the necessary modifications would be carried out by Jadepoint Engineering. Of course, this work merely deferred the sad day when the faithful turboprop would finally be retired, so both the Franco-Italian ATR.42 and the BAe ATP were being evaluated as a possible longer term solution.

Shortage of capacity during the summer underlined the need for additional aircraft, so it was fortunate that in August 1985 Euroair decided to dispose of its four Viscounts to the Southend-based company for £2.5 million. They were quickly repainted in BAF's livery and were the first of the fleet to appear with 'British' in large letters along the fuselage, a practice previously favoured by British Airways. When the flag carrier decided to drop the idea, BAF immediately adopted it for its own purposes.

Two of the Viscount 806s did not receive this treatment because they were sold to the new Spanish airline *Lineas Aereas Canarias* which intended operating inter-island schedules in the Canaries. The remarkably good price of £3 million was obtained for the pair, with the deal including both maintenance and a spares back-up package. The sale certainly boosted the BAF Group's profitability, but it was by no means the only source of income. Under Jadepoint the leasing business begun by the Keegan Group had continued and now had aircraft placed with British Caledonian, British Midland Airways, Manx Airlines, Virgin Atlantic and Janus Airways. This activity alone was expected to produce a turnover in excess of £4 million during the financial year ending in March 1986.

While such results were most welcome, probably one of the most important events in BAF's 1985 calendar came with the launch of its first international scheduled service to link Gatwick with Rotterdam. To ease the onward travel arrangements rail tickets for the Gatwick Express were sold during the course of the journey which was made three times Monday to Friday and once on Saturday and Sunday. Later in the year an early morning departure from the UK was introduced in response to passenger demand, with the change accompanied by the appearance of a welcome hot breakfast for the early starters.

Serious problems were experienced with advance bookings due to KLM's refusal to allow the airline access to the CORDA computer systems. Dutch travel agents were also denied access to BAF reservations which proved an insurmountable difficulty in marketing the route. It meant a serious loss of traffic for the British carrier, so in an attempt to remedy the impact, a fourth service was provided on 1st October. Fares were also trimmed in the face of the fierce competition, but it was a situation which could not continue indefinitely. Despite all possible efforts, passenger levels continued to fall, until by early 1987, a Shorts 360 had replaced the Viscount on the route. Even with all its 35 seats filled, the yield was still far from satisfactory, leaving little alternative but to end the operation on 1st May after two hard years of perseverance.

Undoubtedly it was a disappointment for the airline but by no means a disaster. Long before the decision was taken to withdraw from the Dutch route, preparations for a new venture were already well advanced. The airline's latest project involved the south coast airport at Southampton, where a base was to be set up to offer scheduled services to the Channel Islands. This link had been provided by British Island (BIA)/Air UK for many years, but with the Government's more liberal approach to competing air services, the route became one of the first to benefit.

BAF announced that the proposed £29 fare would be the cheapest available, yet remain fully bookable in either direction. At first a minimum of four daily return flights by 30-seat Shorts 330s were planned, supplemented at weekends by the larger capacity Viscounts. A record number of advance bookings were received by the airline's reservation department, confirming the belief that neither the public nor travel trade were in favour of complicated and restrictive fare structures.

All augured well for the new venture, which was launched on Thursday, 2nd April 1987, after being purposely delayed by 24 hours to avoid the inevitable April Fool jokes from within the airline industry. A daily Southampton-Manchester service was started on the same day, while the frequency of the existing flights between the north west airport and the Channel Islands was doubled. Even at this early stage success seemed assured, especially when the airline found it necessary to add another 2,000 seats over the Easter weekend, which in turn produced the optimistic yet plausible forecast that some 325,000 passengers would be carried in the first year.

Sadly, it was a statistic that was never proved. While there was no shortage of customers, problems began to manifest themselves within the company. In August it was admitted that the airline was suffering from a cash flow problem and was in urgent need of some capital investment. In the absence of a benefactor, the only solution was to sell one of the assets, preferably one for which there was an interested customer.

For this reason Guernsey Airlines was sold to Aurigny Aviation Holdings for an undisclosed sum, with the negotiations concluded on 6th August 1987. Handover of the company was arranged for 1st October, but no aircraft were involved because all of those employed were leased from the parent company. From the outset the new owner indicated that it would not be maintaining the Southampton route from the island, a sector which BAF considered to be more viable than any other in the UK. It was expected it to make between £11,000 and £20,000 profit in the first year, but this estimate was disputed by Aurigny. Unhappily, under the terms of the contract BAF was prevented from flying schedules between the two points to the detriment of Southampton airport. The latter had enjoyed the brief surge of traffic for the past few months, but suddenly the welcome additional income from the regular movements had evaporated overnight.

At least the money raised by the sale helped BAF in the short term, but by the end of the year the airline was again in difficulty. With the cutback in the number of schedules flown, some of the Viscounts were declared surplus and available for sale. Confirmation had been received from the CAA that the life extension programme was proceeding on course, making the aircraft an attractive proposition for any small carrier in search of a reliable

Inside the maintenance hangar at Southend, a Baltic Viscount receives attention.
British World

The amalgamation of BAF with Baltic Airlines in 1988 also involved the latter's associate company which traded as Hot Air using Viscount G-BAPF.
via British World

and economic transport for an outlay of about £1 million, compared with over £12 million for a new 70-seat turboprop. At this point BAF was still expecting to operate 12 Viscounts, three Heralds, four '330s and one '360 in the following summer season, but hardly had the New Year begun when an unseasonable announcement brought an element of gloom to the airline.

ADMINISTRATION AND BEYOND

On 8th January 1988, the company sought to go under Administration, the British equivalent of the US Chapter 11 bankruptcy protection facility. Ironically, the airline had always been profitable, but it was in its present plight because of losses sustained by other elements of the Jadepoint Group. Following the application, the High Court duly appointed the chartered accountants Touche Ross to manage BAF's affairs until a buyer was found. The appearance of these unknown sums specialists at the Southend headquarters initially produced an air of deep depression and apprehension amongst the work force, but once it was realised that the carrier was continuing to trade successfully, the despair gave way to enthusiastic support. Indeed, without the guidance of the Administrators and the staff who faithfully remained with BAF throughout the unsettled period, it is most unlikely that the airline would have reached its 50th anniversary.

This display of loyalty helped to convince the industry that the setback was only temporary, resulting in numerous expressions of encouragement from satisfied customers. One of the most valuable came with an extension to the contract held with Shell, which kept three Viscounts permanently employed at Aberdeen for the regular oil rig crew change flights to and from Sumburgh. A further demonstration of confidence was given by the US parcels carrier, Federal Express, when it selected the Southend-based airline to provide the feeder links between Heathrow and its European hub at Brussels. The night newspaper distribution contract for Higgs Air Agency also continued.

Although BAF had discontinued its own scheduled services towards the end of the previous year, the company still operated the Gatwick-Maastricht, Luton-Maastricht and Luton-Dublin sectors on behalf of Virgin Atlantic with dedicated Viscounts. Various short term leases were also undertaken during the period, all contributing to the survival factor. It was therefore with some satisfac-

tion that the Administrators announced on 28th October that BAF was likely to become the first major British company to be rescued under the 1986 Insolvency Act. An agreement had been reached whereby the assets of the carrier and its engineering subsidiary would be acquired by Mostjet Ltd, a holding company formed specifically for the purpose. The deal was considered to be good news for the creditors, the 350 or so work force and for Southend airport, while it also helped to reassure customers, both new and old, that BAF could be relied upon to sustain current contracts and handle any future business.

Negotiations also involved the participation of another carrier, namely Baltic Airlines. When formed at the Essex airport in early 1988 it was also equipped with Viscounts, in this case the five aircraft were Series 810s previously with British Midland and Manx. A number of ex-BAF personnel were recruited which began contract and *ad hoc* charter work, the latter operated under the title Hot Air. Several of Baltic's directors were involved in the creation of Mostjet during the year, so when the deal with BAF was agreed, it included the amalgamation of the two companies and the integration of the fleet, taking the total to 20 Viscounts, 14 of which were operational, plus two Heralds. In addition, a number of contracts were transferred, one being the operation of a feeder service for Swissair between Dakar (Senegal) and Banjul (Gambia).

Nevertheless, for a time the October announcement appeared to be a little premature because it was not until 3rd May 1989 that the restructuring process was finalised and BAF was able to emerge from Administration. Both the Inland Revenue and the CAA had played a part in the delay, each raising objections for different reasons. The tax officials were eventually satisfied, while the fears that the airline could possibly come under foreign control resolved themselves when the Swedish investor Lennart Hesselburg withdrew his interest.

Mostjet's chief executive, Ian Herman, in reviewing BAF's prospects, said that its charter activities were very satisfactory and filled an important niche in the market. The two all-cargo Viscounts on strength were also busy and the airline was keen to develop its freight operations still further, especially with the rapid expansion of the express parcels and courier business in Europe. Overall it was expected that the Group turnover for 1989 would exceed £25 million. As a part of the re-organisation, not only did BAF

One-Eleven 201AC G-DBAF was one of three acquired by BAF in early 1990 for IT work. It was originally delivered to British United at Gatwick in July 1965 registered G-ASJG. After several years of operations it was put into store at Southend.
Jean Wright

Flown in an all-white livery with BAF titles, the BAe 146-200QC G-BTIA served with the airline in 1991-92, before returning to the manufacturer in August prior to joining a South African airline.
Author

In the early 1990s BAF was one of the airlines contracted to operate feeder flights for Federal Express, using Fokker F.27 Friendships supplied by the US carrier. In BAF's case the airline operated G-FEAD for the work, which ended in 1992.
Author

Spirited flypast by Viscount 806 G-AOYR at Southend. Named 'Viscount Gatwick', it carries the large 'British' title adopted by BAF after British Airways dropped the use of this identity.
via British World

intend to upgrade its corporate identity, but the large investment programme included the possibility of adding jet equipment to the fleet.

It was Spring 1990 before there were any obvious signs of expansion which was marked by the arrival of three somewhat elderly one-time British United One-Elevens. The machines had been in the US since the early 1980s, serving such carriers as Pacific Express and Braniff before returning the their homeland. In the event only two of the trio were flown on BAF's services, but were completely refurbished with a 78-seat interior to give a high standard of comfort.

After several years work the One-Elevens were retired for storage at Southend, but in the meantime the airline had announced that it had taken delivery of a BAe 146-200QC (QC – Quick Change), thereby renewing its association with the type eight years or so after carrying out the route proving trials for the manufacturer. This QC variant was intended to open up new markets for the airline since the aircraft was equipped with a large cargo door to facilitate use in either a passenger or freight role. BAF Engineering was responsible for its maintenance, a useful addition to its capabilities in view of the planned introduction of the type at nearby London City in 1992. BAF's chairman, Robert Sturman, anticipated that the airline could become regular users of the Docklands airport, but subsequently the two 146s on strength later became fully committed to other regular work.

In November 1991 BAF acquired the services of a new managing director, Neil Hansford, the former general manager, airline marketing with TNT Express Worldwide. During the nine years with the company, he was responsible for setting up the freighter network employing 18 BAe 146s to serve 38 European airports. With this experience of a market ideally suited to BAF's operations, it seemed likely that Hansford would be able to further develop this aspect of the airline's activities. Interestingly, in a statement made at the time of his appointment, he referred to the expansion of charter and scheduled services that were outside the scope of TNT. No details were forthcoming at that stage, but at least it gave an indication of his future plans for BAF.

One of these was revealed in March when the news was released that the company was to become the only British airline to operate a dedicated Boeing 747 freighter. This impressive step was to be taken in association with the US supplemental cargo carrier Evergreen International, which would be supplying both crew and aircraft in the first instance. However, it was intended that at some time in the future the operation would become entirely British, but in the meantime a new jointly owned company formed as Evergreen International Europe Ltd would be responsible for the project.

Although administration would be handled at Southend, obviously the airport could not accommodate a 747, therefore an alternative operating base had to be found. No decision had been reached, but Manston was favoured because of its size and position, plus the fact that it already handled a considerable amount of freight traffic. Unfortunately, before any positive steps could be taken, Evergreen decided against the arrangement, so disappointingly, a 747 was never repainted in BAF's livery.

A second innovative scheme also failed to materialise, this time due to lack of official approval. A much-needed courier service, offering guaranteed letter, packet and parcel deliveries , appropriately branded 'Orient Express', was planned to link Hong Kong with Singapore six nights per week. The one-off One-Eleven freighter variant was earmarked for the regular trips, which would have been timed so that connections could be made with every major south east Asian city. Although a start-up date was provisionally arranged, no flights were operated in the absence of the necessary licence.

Overall, 1992 was a difficult year for the Mostjet companies. After a good start, BAF suffered a severe setback when Federal Express decided to withdraw from Europe. It was particularly disappointing because the staff had worked hard to build up a very good relationship with the US carrier, which was very impressed with the performance achieved by the Viscount. The loss of this business brought the need for a significant reduction in the number of aircrew employed, which in turn affected the amount of maintenance work carried out by the Engineering division.

Fortunately, the IT work was thriving to such an extent that it was necessary to lease a pair of Boeing 727s from Yugoslav Airlines (JAT). This action aroused some adverse comment from the British airline industry, but after only two months or so, the tri-jets had to be returned in order to comply with UN sanctions imposed on the participants in the latest war. Nevertheless, there had to be replacements, so two Adria Airways McDonnell Douglas MD-82s flew BAF's services from Gatwick throughout the summer.

There was a bright end to the year when the airline began work on the newly-won Parcel Force contract, which called for nightly flights between Edinburgh and Coventry. About the same time the entire 11-strong Dan-Air One-Eleven 500 fleet was moved to Southend following the sad demise of the airline. It was planned to keep five of the aircraft in service to cover the booming IT, *ad hoc* charter and leasing business forecast for 1993, while another four were stored under a care and maintenance agreement pending possible resale. The remaining pair unselfishly donated various parts for the welfare of their more fortunate colleagues, a fate later shared by another of the batch. This left three to be overhauled prior to their sale to customers in South Africa and Nigeria in 1995.

Nevertheless, despite all the problems, BAF was still one of the few profitable European airlines, although the management warned that for this to continue, flexibility was essential. It meant that constant changes had to be accepted if business was not to be lost to the competition, but few realised that the airline's name was not immune and that British Air Ferries was destined to disappear in the coming months. During the course of a long and illustrious career it had witnessed the end of well over one hundred large and small, well known and unknown airlines, yet BAF had survived a similar fate. British World would build on this record to continue the same high standard of service, efficiency and reliability.

The Leaping Lion

Welcome aboard! With the new image of British World and the 'leaping lion' logo, crew uniforms and interior decor were given an new look. To underline BWA's approach to its work, the phrase 'Chartering Excellence' was devised, well emphasising the airline's intent.
British World

On 6th April 1993 a famous name in British aviation ceased to exist. Its place had been taken by British World Airlines (BWA), a title considered to be more appropriate for the company and one which finally removed the car ferry image. Almost 20 years after the last vehicle had been carried across the Channel, the airline still received an occasional enquiry about the service. Changing a long-established identity is never easy and is an expensive exercise not to be taken lightly, but in this case it was considered worthwhile. Coinciding with this re-organisation, Mostjet Ltd became British World Aviation Ltd, a name thought more suitable for the Group's holding company.

At the relaunch it was announced that BWA would be adopting an entirely new strategy to develop its business worldwide. Henceforth marketing would place a greater emphasis on passenger flying, which in any case already accounted for some 70% of the carrier's revenue. It was also confirmed that Stansted would become the company's operation's centre, with administration remaining in Viscount House at Southend. In reality turboprop flights had been gradually moving to London's third airport for several months preceding the change of identity, mainly because there were fewer restrictions for the growing number of night freight operations.

Naturally, it was impossible to complete the transformation overnight, but gradually over a period of a few months the aircraft livery, cabin interiors, staff uniforms, signs and stationery all displayed the new lion logo. The 12 Viscounts in the fleet proved an exception because after the first example (G-BFZL) had been repainted in the latest scheme, the remainder were either given the all-red finish stipulated by the Parcel Force contracts, or were running out of hours before a major check was due. Since the latter is now becoming increasingly expensive to carry out, when aircraft reach this landmark they will be retired. As a compromise, all were given the revised titles but otherwise retained their BAF colours.

The opportunity was also taken to update operating procedures, while various passenger service improvements were implemented, ranging from check-in to in-flight catering. Historically, charter carriers tend to be less well known to the travelling public compared with those operating schedules, mainly because the vast majority book a holiday which includes the flight arrangements in the package. Tour operators' brochures certainly include a small section devoted to the airborne element of the journey, but usually they list almost every airline still operational together with the names of most of the civil airliner types currently in service! With so little publicity it is not surprising that carriers often do not receive the recognition they deserve. Hopefully, BWA will enjoy a greater public awareness in its new guise.

Tour operators Air Style and Travel Club of Upminster were two of the companies using the Stansted-based One-Eleven and BAe 146-300 during the 1993 summer season, while an example of each type also operated from Manchester. These mainly covered the needs of Owners Abroad, Barwell Travel and The Air Travel Group. In the south, the airline out-stationed two aircraft at Gatwick, the customers being principally Flight Directors and Goldcrest.

At the beginning of the year it had been predicted that there would be a late surge in holiday bookings as the country's economic situation showed signs of improvement. This proved to be

an accurate forecast which resulted in BWA being
contracted for over 2,000 flights between May and
October. Additional capacity again became necessary and was met by the lease of the Adria MD-82s
once more, their appearance naturally sparking
off another spate of criticism from the industry.

SCHEDULES

Hardly had these developments been digested
when news was released that the airline had applied for traffic rights for a scheduled service between Stansted and Bucharest. This appeared to
confirm the managing director's interest in this
form of activity despite the carrier's past experi-
ences. The Romanian venture proposed to offer
One-Eleven 500 flights departing at 1130 hours
on Monday, Wednesday and Friday, arriving back

at 1910 hours. At first the service was planned for
start-up on 24th May, but this had to be post-
poned for a month or so until the necessary ap-
provals were obtained. Finally, all was ready for
the inaugural flight on Monday, 28th June, when
BWA became the first British airline to link the
two countries since British Airways (BA) pulled
off the route in the early 1980s.

One of the recently refurbished 99-seat One-
Elevens (G-OBWD) was employed, with the
cabin divided into Economy and the new World
Class sections. Those travelling in the latter accommodation were given menus for the multi-
course meal provided during the flight, but the
same high level of attention and service was afforded all passengers. The choice of destination
was unusual, but enormous opportunities were

available in Eastern Europe, it was felt that an alternative to the Romanian flag carrier's schedule would be welcomed by those visiting Bucharest on business. After the first month of operation, the airline reported that excellent loads were being carried from Stansted, but an increase in frequency was restricted by a bilateral agreement between the UK and Romania. This problem was overcome by December when it became feasible to add a Sunday rotation, with extra flights provided over the Christmas period.

Despite the apparent success, there was still a great need to publicise the availability of the non-stop service. From habit many business travellers continued to depart from Heathrow before 0800 hours for the five hour journey to Bucharest which even involved an intermediate aircraft change. As a result they were unable to appreciate BWA's superior World Class when compared with the Business Class service offered by other European airlines. As if this was not enough, for good measure the British carrier's fares were several hundred pounds cheaper. Any of these factors should have been sufficient to ensure success, but although load factors were quite good, yields were too low. Passengers tended to be those looking for the cheapest possible fare and were very often members of charities involved in relief work in Romania. In addition, competing with Tarom was difficult because the latter's costs were much lower. Eventually, in the face of mounting losses, the decision was taken to discontinue the schedule in Spring 1994 after one year of endeavour.

Bucharest had been planned to be the first of several similar cities that BWA hoped to introduce to its scheduled network. These were to be added at intervals over the next few years, but circumstances changed the programme to some extent. Within three months of the Romanian launch the carrier decided to serve Lourdes, following BA's

decision to drop the route. It was envisaged that a weekend service would be provided, possibly in association with Tangney Tours, but despite a number of discussions, the scheme failed to materialise. The tour operator favoured Gatwick as the British gateway for a thrice-weekly service, but this was unacceptable to the airline.

Two significant events occurred around the turn of the year, both involving the airline's management team. In December 1993, Mike Kay re-

BAC One-Eleven 518 on the apron at Bucharest. Although the Romanian route lasted less than a year, it proved BWA's scheduled capabilities.
Author

signed his post of commercial director after being responsible for many of the innovative schemes introduced through the years. Early in the New Year it was announced that the managing director, Neil Hansford, had also left the company. Neil wished to pursue his ambition to establish an airline offering domestic and European routes from regional airports. The result was Euro Direct, which sadly fell by the wayside in February 1995 after less than a year of operations.

**Backbone of BWA's present day fleet are
five BAC One-Eleven Series 500s, giving the
airline an enviable flexibility.**
Glen Sweeney / British World

WORLD AVIATION SUPPORT

Ever since the Keegan Group created BAF Engineering in 1973, the company has been responsible for the welfare of the associated airline's fleet. Over 20 years later it still resides in the two north-side hangars vacated by Channel Airways at the time of its collapse in 1972, but the complex now includes extensive workshop and specialised overhaul and maintenance areas, together with training schools and offices.

When Keegan sold the airline operations to Jadepoint in 1983, the original deal did not include the engineering division, but within a short time this omission was rectified and the unit became Jadepoint Aircraft Engineering. Five years or so later it reverted to BAF Engineering, a title it retained even when its fellow Group member became British World Airlines (BWA) in April 1993. Although the airline was in the process of moving most of its operations to Stansted, its engineering associate had no such plans and intended to stay at Southend into the future. With some 250 employees, it was a successful company in its own right, but had taken the precaution of seeking third party work rather than rely entirely upon BWA for its income, although this still accounted for some 60% of the total. By expanding the range of types covered to include the Douglas DC-9 and Boeing 737 variants, the dependence on the airline was reduced to about 50%.

Despite the earlier intention, in September 1993 BAF Engineering ceased to exist, its place taken by World Aviation Support (WAS). One of its first successes under its new identity was a three year contract to maintain the three BAC One-Elevens of Cyprus Airways. At the time it was the largest ever won by the company, but other overseas work was under active negotiation. Nearer home, a five year agreement with TNT Express Worldwide was signed in early 1994,

with WAS becoming responsible for the maintenance of the carrier's BAe 146 fleet. As a consequence, a new overhaul base was opened at London's third airport which could house three '146s at one time, those of TNT being joined by BWA's and British Aerospace Defence. It elevated WAS into the position of the largest independent

146 third party engineering organisation in Europe with 18 aircraft under contract.

Staff at Southend were reassured by the news that the unit's workload would be unchanged with both the One-Eleven and Viscount maintenance remaining at the original facility. Some of the engineers with the company had spent most of their working lives in the two hangars albeit with different employers. Many witnessed the

Not surprisingly, World Aviation Support has developed a considerable speciality in the BAC One-Eleven. This example, a flying test-bed in the colours of the Royal Aerospace Establishment, now the Defence Evaluation and Research Agency.
via British World

A good spectrum of the types that WAS can encompass, from Beech Baron light twins (left, centre), to executive jets (in this case a Lear Jet, foreground) to jet airliners (BAC One-Elevens).
Glen Sweeney / British World

Crowded hangar scene at WAS Southend.
via British World

introduction of the Viscount and have subsequently helped to keep the veterans in pristine condition. Indeed, the type is regarded with great affection and few will not regret its passing when the time comes for final retirement. But hopefully, that date is some time away.

Although younger in years, the One-Elevens have had busy lives flying IT charters for much of their careers, so a comprehensive programme of refurbishment was carried out by WAS after they arrived at Southend. When completed, the spacious, fully carpeted cabin had a wide-bodied appearance complete with overhead lockers and attractive decor. An adjustable curtain can divide the Club Class accommodation as required, with in-flight service arranged accordingly. The transformation produced many complimentary remarks from passengers pleasantly surprised with the high standard achieved, which was certainly a credit to the engineering division.

Although BWA plans to continue operating the One-Eleven 500s for the next few years, in 2002 the type will have to be retired from European operations due the implementation of the Stage 2 noise regulations. No decision has been taken about possible hush-kitting, an expensive and performance restricting undertaking. Since compulsory retirement is not imminent, the airline is going to monitor developments carefully before spending a considerable sum of money on aircraft it might not be operating in six years time. However, if hush-kitting becomes viable the task will no doubt be entrusted to WAS.

MAJOR CONTRACTS

In late 1993, BWA won a valuable contract from the Ministry of Defence (MoD) to carry military personnel and their families between the UK and various bases in Germany. Britannia Airways had operated the flights for a number of years from Luton with Boeing 737s, but with the latter type being phased out of the fleet, the carrier no longer had suitable equipment for the duties. Undoubtedly, the contract was a major development for BWA since it was worth about £12 million over a three year period commencing in April 1994. A BAe 146-300 configured with 110 seats was earmarked for the operation, the type's versatility playing a large part in the success of the airline's tender.

The flights, which are at least daily, link Stansted with RAF Bruggen, Hanover, Paderborn and Munster, with the majority of passengers being families starting or ending leave periods. Since a good proportion are children, it was necessary for an alternative to be offered to replace the video programmes provided by Britannia for in-flight entertainment. The contract specified that 'kiddypacks' would be available for the amusement of the junior citizens onboard, each bag containing

drawing and colouring implements, together with games and novelties.

In addition, BWA also operates numerous *ad hoc* sorties for the MoD, although these are usually booked at least one month in advance. The flights are needed for troop change-over movements, which can involve the transportation of 100 or so fully-armed personnel in battle fatigues. Although Stansted is often used, there is actually no fixed departure point for these charters, with the traffic handled by various airports scattered around the United Kingdom.

cles of the huge Parcel Force operation, developing both the operation and aircraft in order to further improve turn-around times wherever possible, so the award was accepted with pleasure. In common with various carriers similarly employed, the regular night runs are flown throughout the year regardless of weather conditions, which can be very unpleasant.

The summer season proved to be very successful for the carrier, but the next year promised to be even better. Well before the start of the 1995 programme, the sales and marketing director, Mike

In June 1994 BWA learned that it had become one of the initial winners of the Post Office's First Class Awards. These had been instigated to emphasise the new customer-focused structure and to reward key businesses and accredited suppliers for the quality of service achieved during the year. This prestigious award was won again by BWA in 1995.

British World received an award from The Air Travel Group for on-time performance during 1994. This was a contributory factor in their awarding BWA a contract worth £5.6 million for flying in the summer of 1995. This represented BWA's largest IT charter contract to date.

BWA had worked for the Post Office for many years, its aircraft carrying the same distinctive all-red colour scheme as adopted by the road vehi-

Sessions, was able to announce that BWA was already fully committed for the forthcoming season. Up to 1,100 seats per day were available to cope with the expected 25% increase in the number of IT passengers carried. All of this clearly confirmed the carrier's long-held belief that the smaller tour operators preferred the flexibility of 100-seat aircraft.

In addition to this type of work, the airline has become a major source of extra capacity by supplying aircraft to the larger carriers in busy periods. Many of the latter have been forced to trim their fleets in the face of financial obligations, so short-term leases provide the answer. One such customer has been SABENA which used a '146 during 1994 to operate the links between Scotland and Brussels. On the strength of this satisfactory

During 1996 the BAe 146-300 G-BTZN was the sole example of the type in the BWA fleet. It has served since April 1994.
Author

A happy band of tour operators and others within the travel business after sampling the BWA One-Eleven 500 service. Series 520 G-OBWC is one of five in operation.
Glen Sweeney / British World

The Viscounts supplied to the Parcel Force operation are a good example of the capabilities of BWA. Flown to exacting schedules and in all weathers, they are central to the success of the nationwide service. Series 806 G-PFBT entered service with BAF in April 1981 as G-AOYP.
Glen Sweeney / British World

arrangement, the airline contracted BWA to supply a One-Eleven for the entire 1995 summer, this time for scheduled service work between Brussels and other European cities. In order to comply with the customer's requirements, it meant that two aircraft had to be allocated to the duties so that the regular maintenance periods could be covered without a break. Both machines had their previous livery removed with SABENA's title carried by the operational machine.

Undoubtedly, the One-Eleven has proved itself ideal for this type of business because its low capital cost enables BWA to offer attractive rates to would-be customers. Services can also be operated for a newly-formed airline with limited resources, thereby avoiding the expense of acquiring its own equipment until the enterprise has proved to be viable.

Of course, such employment means that an aircraft is often committed to a specific contract, which with only five One-Elevens in the fleet, requires some careful planning. One solution is to lease in aircraft as in the past, or alternatively to expand the fleet to meet the growth of the IT charter market. This latter course was chosen by BWA during 1995, resulting in a careful review of types considered suitable for the airline's needs. Eventually the Boeing 737-200 was selected and a possible source identified for the lease of three examples of the breed. Deliveries were provisionally set for the start of the 1996 summer programme, the final decision dependent upon the support of the tour operators. In the event the venture was abandoned before any positive steps had been taken, in part due to the unacceptably high charges now demanded for 737s, but mainly because the expected growth was not in evidence. A general decline in the European leisure market meant that tour operators large and small were forced to cut back their programmes to avoid disastrous losses, which in turn affected the number of charter flights contracted. BWA will rely upon its five One-Elevens and single 146 to handle the 1996 IT operations.

These were not the only aircraft likely to join the expanding fleet during the year, because after a lengthy period of evaluation, options were taken on a pair of ATR.72-210s for possible use on the Shell contract at Aberdeen. Since a change of type was proposed by the airline, the oil company invited tenders from interested carriers so that it could carefully consider all proposals, particularly those relating to performance and reliability. Undoubtedly, the three Vis-

counts used for many years fulfilled the task admirably and were very popular with the rig workers, but on the other hand, they were becoming increasingly expensive to operate compared with a new aircraft. BWA was successful in renewing the contract – valued at £55 million – in November 1995, against fierce competition. The order for the two ATR.72s was formally signed at Toulouse on 15th January in the presence of Robert Sturman from BWA and Henri-Paul Puel, Chief Executive Officer of the newly-created Aero International (Regional) Anglo-French-Italian consortium. The first was delivered on 28th March to enable it to enter service on 2nd April. It was planned that its companion would follow by early June.

The new Shell UK Exploration and Production support contract will mean the withdrawal of the Viscounts from the Scottish outstation and effectively the end of the type's passenger activities in the UK. During their time based at Sumburgh 1.5 million passengers had been carried up to the winning of the new contract with a dispatch reliability of 98%. The Viscount has indeed been a very faithful servant.

Those with a reasonable life expectancy will be converted into freighters, but before this stage is reached, BWA plan to operate a series of special trips to commemorate the end of a long era. Through the years, the airline has always given generous support to enthusiasts' organisations including the donation of Herald 100 G-APWA to the Herald Society for display at the Museum of Berkshire Aviation at Woodley and Viscount G-APIM to the Brooklands Museum at Weybridge.

Another group not forgotten by BWA comprises customers and suppliers. From time to time the airline arranges a day trip to some destination on the continent as a way of expressing the thanks of the company for the support given. These outings usually include a visit to local points of interest followed by lunch, with time for shopping before the return flight. These gestures are much appreciated by those invited and undoubtedly helps to keep the airline's name to the forefront.

Now that BWA is concentrating its efforts on the market it knows well, it can cautiously look forward to a future full of promise. All too often carriers become too ambitious too early in their careers, quickly suffering the consequences. No one can accuse British World Airlines of such impatience, but the reward has been to reach its half century, no mean feat in the turbulent airline industry.

A new era. G-OILA, the first of two
ATR.72-210s in full British World colours
on the ramp at Toulouse just before
delivery, March 1996. Note the French test
registration F-WWEJ and line no. 472 on
the rear fuselage.
AI(R)

Above: **Freighter Mk 32 G-APAU served the group from 1957 to 1971.** Below: **Viscount 806 G-BLOA in freight guise carried 'Freightmaster' titles with BAF.** Both Author

50 Years of Variety

As might be imagined, 50 years of continuous operation in a wide variety of manners has produced an impressive list of aircraft types. This includes aircraft operated at one time or another by companies which have played a part in the history of British World Airlines. While every attempt has been made to ensure its accuracy, inevitably there will be some omissions due to short-term leases or sub charters that have gone unrecorded.

Aircraft are listed by type, then by registration, sub-type or variant (if applicable), date of acquisition, operator (in sequence if more than one), then details of disposal or status.

Abbreviations

AK - Air Kruise, BAF - British Air Ferries, BRI - Britavia, BTC - Baltic Airlines, BU - British United Air Ferries, BWA - British World Airlines, CAB - Air Charter/Channel Air Bridge, CAT - Cie Air Transport, Dbr - Damaged beyond repair, GER - Guernsey Airlines, JER - Jersey Air Ferries, SCA - Silver City Airways, Scr - Scrapped, WO - Written off.

Airspeed AS.65 Consul

G-AHRK	–	9.49	SC	Sold in Spain 4.52 as EC-AGI
G-AIBF	–	8.46	SC	Scrapped Blackbushe 4.54
G-AIUS	–	2.47	AK, SC	Sold in Morocco 9.58 as CN-TEJ

Aviation Traders ATL.98 Carvair

G-ANYB	–	2.62	CAB, BU, BAF	Scrapped at Lydd 8.70
G-AOFW	–	4.65	BU, BAF	Scrapped at Southend 1.84
G-APNH	–	1.65	BU, BAF	Dbr at Le Touquet 18.3.71
G-AREK	–	4.72	BAF	To CAT as F-BHMV, returned. Sold in France 6.77 as F-BYCL
G-ARSD	–	4.62	CAB, BU, BAF	Scrapped at Lydd 8.70
G-ARSF	–	7.62	CAB	Written off at Rotterdam 28.12.62
G-ASDC	–	3.63	BU, BAF	Sold in the USA 4.79 as N80FA
G-ASHZ	–	7.63	BU, BAF	Sold in the USA 6.79 as N89FA
G-ASKD	–	6.73	BAF	Sold in Norway 10.74 as LN-NAA
G-ASKG	–	8.63	BU, BAF	To CAT as F-BRPT, returned. Sold in Gabon 2.75 as TR-LUP
G-ASKN	–	2.64	BU, BAF	Sold in Gabon 6.76 as TR-LWP
G-ATRV	–	3.66	BU	To CAT as F-BOSU 5.67
G-AXAI	–	4.69	BAF	Sold in France 1.76 as F-BVEF

Avions de Transport Régional ATR.72

G-OILA	-210	3.96	BWA	Current
G-OILB	-210	5.96	BWA	Current

Avro 691 Lancastrian

G-AHBT	Mk III	10.46	SCA	Sold to Skyways 7.47
G-AHBV	Mk III	10.46	SCA	Sold to Skyways 3.49.
G-AHBW	Mk III	10.46	SCA	Sold in Australia 1.48 as VH-EAV

BAC One-Eleven

G-AZUK	-476	4.91	BAF	Returned to lessor 1994
G-DBAF	-201	3.90	BAF	Sold 1995
G-OBWA	-518	12.92	BAF, BWA	Current
G-OBWB	-518	12.92	BAF, BWA	Current
G-OBWC	-520	12.92	BAF, BWA	Current
G-OBWD	-518	1.93	BAF, BWA	Current
G-OBWE	-531	4.93	BAF, BWA	Current
G-OCNW	-201	5.90	BAF	Scrapped at Southend 1995
G-SURE	-416	9.82	BAF	Op for Air Manchester to 11.82

British Aerospace 146

G-BTIA	-200QC	6.91	BAF	Returned to BAe 8.92
G-BRAB	-300	8.92	BWA	Returned to BAe 11.94
G-BTNU	-300	3.93	BWA	Returned to BAe 11.93
G-BTZN	-300	4.94	BWA	Current
G-OBAF	-100	5.82	BAF	Route proving trials for BAe 1982

Breguet Br 761S Deux Ponts

F-BASL		6.53	SCA	Returned to Breguet 9.53

Bristol 170 Freighter

G-AGVB	Srs 21	11.48	SCA	To CAT as F-BHVB 2.57
G-AGVC	Srs 21	7.48	SCA	Dbr at Ronaldsway 30.6.62
G-AHJC	Srs 21	9.48	SCA	Returned to Bristol 11.48
G-AHJD	Srs 21	5.59	SCA	Returned to lessor 1959
G-AHJG	Srs 21	10.47	SCA	Returned to Bristol 1948
G-AHJI	Srs 21	12.55	SCA, AK, BU	Scrapped at Southend 11.65
G-AHJJ	Srs 21	2.50	SCA	Written off at Cowbridge 21.3.50
G-AHJO	Srs 21	9.48	SCA	Returned to lessor 1949
G-AHJP	Srs 21	3.51	SCA	Sold in Morocco 11.53 as F-DABJ
G-AICM	Srs 21	4.51	SCA	WO at Tempelhof, Berlin 19.1.53
G-AICS	Srs 21	6.52	SCA	WO at Winter Hill, Lancs, 27.2.58
G-AIFM	Srs 21	10.51	SCA	Sold in Morocco 1.54 as F-DABK, returned to AK, SCA, BU. Scrapped at Southend 10.64
G-AIFV	Srs 21	3.50	SCA	Scrapped at Lydd 5.62
G-AIME	Srs 21	11.50	SCA, AK, BU	Scrapped at Southend 5.64
G-AIMH	Srs 21	4.52	SCA	Scrapped at Lydd 1963

Towards the end of its career with BAF, Carvair G-ASDC took on the largely bare metal scheme and the name 'Plain Jane'.
via British World

Boeing 727 YU-AKG was one of two leased from Jugoslav Airlines to meet IT capacity demand in 1992.
Nick Godfrey / British World

When BAF acquired the Dan-Air One-Eleven 500s in late 1992, the aircraft initially operated in a hybrid livery. G-OBWC was the former G-BEKA.
Author

Reg	Type	Date	Operators	Notes
G-AMLP	Srs 32	2.53	CAB, BAF	Sold to Midland Air Cargo 11.70
G-AMSA	Srs 32	2.54	CAB, BU	Scrapped at Lydd 4.67
G-AMWA	Srs 32	3.53	SCA, BU	Written off Guernsey 24.9.63
G-AMWB	Srs 32	4.53	SCA, BU, BAF	Scrapped at Lydd 4.68
G-AMWC	Srs 32	5.53	SCA, BU	Scrapped at Lydd 4.67
G-AMWD	Srs 32	5.53	SCA	To CAT as F-BKBD 4.61, to BU, scrapped at Southend 4.67
G-AMWE	Srs 32	6.53	SCA, BU	Scrapped at Lydd 1967
G-AMWF	Srs 32	6.53	SCA, BU, BAF	Scrapped at Lydd 3.68
G-ANMF	Srs 32	8.54	CAB, BU	Scrapped at Lydd 8.70
G-ANVR	Srs 32	3.55	CAB, BU	Sold to Midland Air Cargo 3.71
G-ANVS	Srs 32	4.55	CAB, BU, BAF	Scrapped at Lydd 7.70
G-ANWG	Srs 32	6.54	SCA	To CAT as F-BKBG 5.61
G-ANWH	Srs 32	7.54	SCA	To CAT as F-BLHH 12.62
G-ANWI	Srs 32	7.54	SCA	To CAT as F-BKBI 6.61
G-ANWJ	Srs 32	6.56	SCA, BU	Scrapped at Lydd 4.70
G-ANWK	Srs 32	6.56	SCA, BU, BAF	Scrapped at Lydd 8.70
G-ANWL	Srs 32	7.56	SCA	Written off Guernsey 1.11.61
G-ANWM	Srs 32	7.56	SCA, BU, BAF	To CAT as F-BPIM 1.68, returned. Scrapped at Lydd 10.70
G-ANWN	Srs 32	7.56	SCA, BU	To CAT as F-BPIN 3.68.
G-AOUU	Srs 32	12.56	CAB, BU	Scrapped at Lydd 5.67
G-AOUV	Srs 32	12.56	CAB	To SABENA 4.57 to 11.59, returned. BU, scr at Lydd 4.68
G-APAU	Srs 32	6.57	CAB	To SABENA 11.59 to 5.62, returned. SCA, BU, BAF. Sold to Midland Air Cargo 3.71
G-APAV	Srs 32	4.57	CAB	To SABENA 6.62 to 9.64, returned. BU, BAF. Sold to Midland Air Cargo 11.70

Canadair CL-44

Reg	Type	Date	Operators	Notes
G-ATZH	D-4	5.72	BAF	Returned to Trans Meridian 7.72
G-AZIN	D-4	3.72	BAF	Returned to Trans Meridian 7.72

De Havilland DH.104 Dove

Reg	Type	Date	Operators	Notes
G-AIWF	Srs 1	6.47	SCA	Sold in S Africa 11.51 as ZS-DFA
G-AKJG	Srs 2	10.47	SCA	Sold 1951
G-AKJP	Srs 1	6.48	SCA	Sold 1.51
G-AOYC	Srs 1	2.59	SCA	To Morton Air Services

De Havilland DH.114 Heron

Reg	Type	Date	Operators	Notes
G-AOZM	Srs 1B	4.57	SCA	Sold in Italy 12.59 as I-AOZM
G-AOZN	Srs 1B	2.57	SCA	Sold 11.59

Douglas DC-3/ C-47 Dakota

Reg	Type	Date	Operators	Notes
G-AGND	Mk 4	2.58	SCA	Leased from Cyprus AW to 8.58
G-AIRG	Mk 3	11.46	SCA	Sold 3.48
G-AIRH	Mk 3	12.46	SCA	Sold 5.48
G-AIWC	Mk 3	4.58	SCA	Sold 2.62
G-AJAU	Mk 3	6.47	SCA	Sold 10.47
G-AJAV	Mk 3	6.47	SCA	Sold 6.50
G-AJRY	Mk3	9.71	BAF	Ex Trans Meridian. Registered to T D Keegan for company use. Sold in S Africa 4.74 as ZS-PTG
G-AJZD	Mk 3	7.47	SCA	Sold 3.48
G-AKII	Mk 3	2.58	SCA	Leased from Cyprus AW to 8.58
G-AKNB	Mk 4	12.59	SCA	To British United 1.62
G-ALPN	Mk 4	11.59	SCA	To British United 1.62
G-AMJU	Mk 4	2.58	SCA	To British United 1.62
G-AMPZ	Mk 4	3.62	SCA	To British United (CI) 11.62
G-AMVC	Mk 4	7.58	SCA	Leased from BKS to 9.58
G-AMWV	Mk 4	10.57	SCA	To British United 1.62
G-AMYV	Mk 4	1.53	SCA, AK, SCA	To British United 1.62
G-AMYX	Mk 4	1.53	SCA, AK, SCA	To British United 1.62
G-AMZB	Mk 4	6.56	AK, SCA	To British United 1.62
G-ANAE	Mk 4	10.57	SCA	To British United 1.62
G-ANLF	Mk 3	4.55	AK, SCA	Sold in Belgium 9.61 as OO-SBH
G-AOBN	Mk 4	4.55	AK, SCA	To British United (CI) 11.62

Douglas DC-4/ C-54 Skymaster

Reg	Type	Date	Operators	Notes
G-ALEP	C-54B	1.49	SCA	Leased to 4.51
G-BANO	DC-4	12.72	BAF	Broken up at Stansted 1973
G-BANP	DC-4	1.73	BAF	To Aviation Traders 6.73

Handley Page HP.81 Hermes

Reg	Type	Date	Operators	Notes
G-ALDG	Mk 4	12.59	SCA	Withdrawn from use 10.62
G-ALDI	Mk 4	10.54	BRI, SCA	Scrapped at Stansted 10.62
G-ALDM	Mk 4	11.56	BRI, SCA	Returned to Air Safaris 10.59
G-ALDP	Mk 4	6.54	BRI, SCA	Scrapped at Stansted 10.62
G-ALDU	Mk 4	5.54	BRI, SCA	Scrapped at Southend 10.62
G-ALDX	Mk 4	5.54	BRI, SCA	Scrapped at Blackbushe 11.59

Handley Page HPR.7 Herald

Reg	Type	Date	Operators	Notes
G-APWA	Srs 100	8.76	BAF	Preserved at Woodley, Berks
G-ASVO	Srs 214	1.77	BAF, GER, BAF	Sold to Channel Express 11.93
G-ATIG	Srs 214	11.89	BAF	Leased to 1.93
G-BAVX	Srs 214	1.77	BAF	Sold to o Channel Express 11.91
G-BCWE	Srs 206	1.75	BAF	Sold in Guatemala 4.88, TG-ASA
G-BCZG	Srs 202	3.75	BAF	Sold in Zaire 4.83 as 9Q-CAH
G-BDFE	Srs 206	7.75	BAF	Sold in Zaire 2.84 as 9Q-CAA
G-BEBB	Srs 214	7.76	BAF	Sold to Channel Express 11.85
G-BDZV	Srs 214	6.76	BAF	Sold in France 9.81 as F-BVFP
G-BEYD	Srs 401	10.77	BAF	Scrapped at Southend 10.84
G-BEYE	Srs 401	11.77	BAF	Scrapped at Southend 2.87
G-BEYF	Srs 401	8.77	BAF	Sold to Channel Express 4.88
G-BEYG	Srs 401	9.77	BAF	Sold in Colombia 11.81 as HK-2701X
G-BEYH	Srs 401	1.78	BAF	Sold in Colombia 12.81 as HK-2702X

Reg	Srs	Date	Operator	Notes
G-BEYJ	Srs 401	12.77	BAF	Sold in Guatemala 1985, TG-ALE
G-BEYK	Srs 401	3.78	BAF	Sold to British Island AW 3.78

Hawker Siddeley HS 748

Reg	Srs	Date	Operator	Notes
G-ATMI	Srs 2	4.71	BAF	Leased from Court Line to 11.71
G-ATMJ	Srs 2	11.70	BAF	Leased from Court Line to 10.71

Shorts 330

Reg	Srs	Date	Operator	Notes
G-BEEO	–	6.87	BAF	Returned 11.88
G-BGNB	—	3.87	BAF	Sold to Fairflight 2.88
G-BHWT	-200	3.87	BAF	Dbr at Southend 11.1.88
G-BITX	-200	12.83	BAF	Leased to GER to 9.87. Sold to Fairflight 2.88
G-BKMU	-200	8.85	GER	Returned to Fairflight 7.87
G-BNYA	-200	3.87	BAF	Returned to Fairflight 6.87

Shorts 360

Reg	Srs	Date	Operator	Notes
G-BLTO	-100	9.86	BAF	Returned to Fairflight 4.87

Vickers Viscount

Reg	Srs	Date	Operator	Notes
EI-AOI	Srs 803	3.70	BAF	Leased from Aer Lingus. Returned 9.71.
G-AOHL	Srs 802	2.81	BAF	Cabin trainer at Southend
G-AOHM	Srs 802	2.81	BAF, BWA	Current
G-AOHT	Srs 802	7.81	BAF	Scrapped at Southend 3.91
G-AOHV	Srs 802	1.81	BAF	Reregistered G-BLNB 6.84
		4.93	BWA	Rereg G-OPFI 3.94, current
G-AOYG	Srs 806	1.84	BAF, GER	Stored at Southend from 12.92
G-AOYH	Srs 806	3.82	BAF	Sold in Canada 7.83 as C-GWPY
		8.85	BAF	Returned as G-BNAA. Scrapped.
G-AOYI	Srs 806	7.81	BAF, GER, BAF	Sold to London European 2.85 as G-LOND. Lsd to BAF 1986-87
G-AOYJ	Srs 806	4.81	BAF, GER, BWA	Reregistered G-BLOA 8.84. Scrapped at Southend
G-AOYL	Srs 806	1.84	BAF	Scrapped at Southend 2.93
G-AOYM	Srs 806	1.84	BAF	Sold in Spain 10.85 as EC-DYC
G-AOYN	Srs 806	2.81	BAF, BWA	Reregistered G-OPAS 10.94. Current
G-AOYO	Srs 806	1.84	BAF	Sold in Spain 9.85 as EC-DXU
G-AOYP	Srs 806	4.81	BAF, JER, BWA	Reregistered G-PFBT 3.94. Current
G-AOYR	Srs 806	1.84	BAF, BWA	Stored at Southend from 1994
G-AOYS	Srs 806	5.81	BAF	Scrapped at Southend 2.85
G-APEX	Srs 806	3.81	BAF	Scrapped at Southend
G-APEY	Srs 806	4.81	BAF, BWA	Current
G-APIM	Srs 806	1.84	BAF	Preserved at Brooklands
G-ARBY	Srs 708	12.61	SCA	To British United 1.62
G-ARER	Srs 708	12.61	SCA	To British United 1.62
G-ARGR	Srs 708	12.61	SCA	To British United 1.62
		9.83	BAF	For GER Scottish contract work. Sold 12.83
G-AVIW	Srs 812	4.73	BAF	Leased from Alidair to 10.73
G-AVJB	Srs 815	9.81	BAF	Sold in Sweden 11.86 as SE-IVY
G-AZNA	Srs 813	8.88	BTC	Sold in Belgium 10.92
G-BAPF	Srs 814	3.88	BTC	Scrapped at Southend 1992
G-BAPG	Srs 814	3.88	BTC	Stored at Southend
G-BBDK	Srs 808	9.83	BAF, BWA	Reregistered G-OPFE 10.94. Current
G-BFZL	Srs 836	11.88	BTC, BAF, BWA	Current
G-BLNB	–	–	–	See G-AOHV
G-BLOA	–	–	–	See G-AOYJ
G-BNAA	–	–	–	See G-AOYH
G-CSZB	Srs 804	11.83	BAF, BWA	Current
G-LOND	–	–	–	See G-AOYI
G-OHOT	Srs 813	3.88	BTC, BAF	Written off 25.2.94
G-OPAS	–	–	–	See G-AOYN
G-OPFE	–	–	–	See G-BBDK
G-OPFI	–	–	–	See G-BLNB
G-PFBT	–	–	–	See G-AOYP

For many years operated by British Midland, Viscount 813 G-AZNA was bought by Baltic Airlines in August 1988. It was employed on the Gambia Air Shuttle for some time before returning to the UK in 1990.
Author

Channel Air Bridge inherited Freighter Mk 32 G-AMLP in 1959 after conversion from a Mk 31. It was later flown by both BUAF and BAF.
Ken Ellis collection

Towards the end of its service with BAF, Herald 214 G-ASVO was painted in the current scheme. In late 1993 it was sold to Channel Express after some 17 years service with the Southend-based airline.
via British World

**Carvair G-ASDC climbing out from
Southend in 1967.**
Author

Carvair G-APNH 'Menai Bridge' on the
ramp at Southend with a fellow Freighter
Mk 32 behind and a Channel Airways
Viscount bringing up the rear. G-APNH
entered service in January 1965 and went
on to serve also in BAF colours.
Ken Ellis collection

Freighter Mk 32 G-ANVR at Coventry, March 1971. That month saw the end of 17 years of faithful service that started with Channel Air Bridge in 1955. 'Victor Romeo' would next serve Midland Air Cargo.
Roy Bonser

Designed as a car ferry, the Carvair also made an excellent freighter, particularly for long and bulky loads. Night time loading scene from the 'bare' aluminium livery era.
via British World

During its 15 years of service with the airline, Herald 214 G-BAVX was flown by a number of operators. It was sold to Channel Express in 1991.
Author

Wearing the first livery applied to BAF's new Herald fleet, Series 202 G-BCZG was the second of the type to be delivered to the airline in 1975 after 13 years in Canada. It was subsequently leased to a number of airlines.
via British World

Guernsey Airlines received Viscount 806 G-AOYG from BAF for use on its impressive scheduled service route network.
via British World

The Shell support contract up at Sumburgh, has seen the Viscount fleet exposed to all weathers. The type has proven to be wholly reliable in this demanding role. The Viscount gave way to the ATR.72 in April 1996.
via British World

BAF carried out the BAe 146's commercial route proving trials for British Aerospace in late 1982 using the appropriately registered G-OBAF. It took part in the Farnborough airshow in that year.
Mike Hooks

Short 360 G-BLTO was leased by BAF in September 1986 primarily for use on the Gatwick-Rotterdam services which did not warrant the capacity offered by the Viscount previously employed. Its stay was relatively short because the company discontinued the route in April 1987, whereupon the aircraft was returned to the lessor.
via British World

Always an attractive aircraft, a pleasant air-to-air study of Viscount 836 G-BFZL, the only example to adopt the British World 'leaping lion' colours.
via British World

Opposite: **British World's commitment to Parcel Force's nationwide distribution service has twice resulted in the receipt of their First Class Supplier award. The Viscounts appear in Parcel Force's striking all-red colours and logos.**
via British World

Above: **The first of two ATR.72-210s, G-OILA, on a test flight from Toulouse, prior to delivery to British World on 28th March 1996. The ATR replaced the Viscount on the Shell Exploration and Production contract, operating out of Sumburgh from early April.**
AI(R)

Work at World Aviation Support goes on around the clock, for the British World fleet and a large number of third party customers. BAC One-Eleven 518 G-OBWB is positioned at WAS's Southend base.
Glen Sweeney / British World

Series 518 G-OBWA entered service in December 1992 and is part of British World's current five-strong fleet.
via British World

**First Series 300 British Aerospace 146
operated by British World was G-BRAB
from August 1992.**
Glen Sweeney / British World

**Current 146-300 with the British World
fleet, G-BTZN, in service from April 1994.**
Author

 This book is dedicated to the employees of British World Airlines – past and present – whose spirit and endeavours have created an operation unique in airline history. With 50 years of experience behind them, they are powerfully equipped for the next half century.